EASY ACOUSTIC GUITAR SONGS

EASY GUITAR WITH NOTES & TAB

2   **STRUM AND PICK PATTERNS**

3   **ABOUT A GIRL**   Nirvana

6   **ACROSS THE UNIVERSE**   The Beatles

10   **AMERICAN PIE**   Don McLean

20   **BLOWIN' IN THE WIND**   Bob Dylan

22   **CRAZY LITTLE THING C...**

24   **FREE BIRD**   Lynyrd Skyn...

28   **THE JOKER**   Steve Miller Band

32   **LANDSLIDE**   Fleetwood Mac / Dixie Chicks

36   **LAYLA**   Eric Clapton

17   **MAGGIE MAY**   Rod Stewart

38   **MIDNIGHT RIDER**   The Allman Brothers Band

44   **MRS. ROBINSON**   Simon & Garfunkel

48   **NAME**   Goo Goo Dolls

39   **ONE HEADLIGHT**   The Wallflowers

52   **ONLY WANNA BE WITH YOU**   Hootie & The Blowfish

56   **SOAK UP THE SUN**   Sheryl Crow

62   **SOMEBODY TO LOVE**   Jefferson Airplane

70   **SUITE: JUDY BLUE EYES**   Crosby, Stills & Nash

76   **TIME IN A BOTTLE**   Jim Croce

65   **WONDERWALL**   Oasis

ISBN 978-1-4234-8082-2

HAL•LEONARD® CORPORATION

7777 W. BLUEMOUND RD. P.O. BOX 13819 MILWAUKEE, WI 53213

For all works contained herein:
Unauthorized copying, arranging, adapting, recording, Internet posting, public performance,
or other distribution of the printed music in this publication is an infringement of copyright.
Infringers are liable under the law.

Visit Hal Leonard Online at
www.halleonard.com

STRUM AND PICK PATTERNS

This chart contains the suggested strum and pick patterns that are referred to by number at the beginning of each song in this book. The symbols ⊓ and ∨ in the strum patterns refer to down and up strokes, respectively. The letters in the pick patterns indicate which right-hand fingers plays which strings.

p = thumb
i = index finger
m = middle finger
a = ring finger

For example; Pick Pattern 2
is played: thumb - index - middle - ring

Strum Patterns   ## Pick Patterns

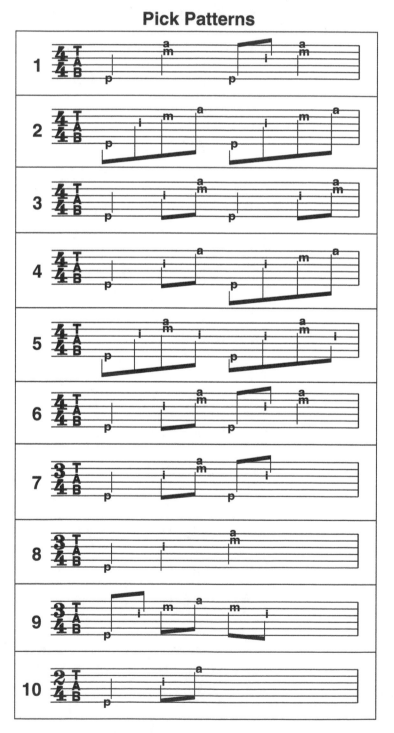

You can use the 3/4 Strum or Pick Patterns in songs written in compound meter (6/8, 9/8, 12/8, etc.). For example, you can accompany a song in 6/8 by playing the 3/4 pattern twice in each measure. The 4/4 Strum and Pick Patterns can be used for songs written in cut time (¢) by doubling the note time values in the patterns. Each pattern would therefore last two measures in cut time.

About a Girl

Words and Music by Kurt Cobain

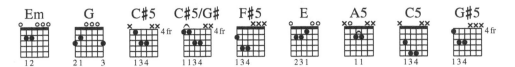

Strum Pattern: 2
Pick Pattern: 4

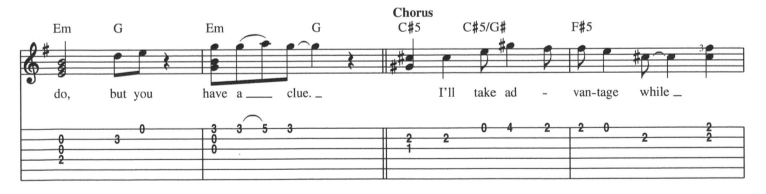

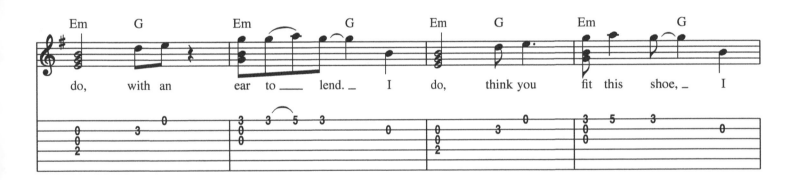

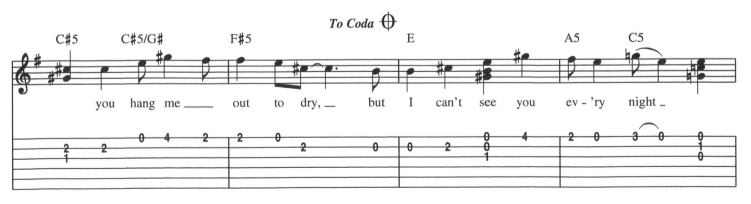

© 1989 THE END OF MUSIC and PRIMARY WAVE TUNES
All Rights Controlled and Administered by EMI VIRGIN SONGS, INC.
All Rights Reserved   International Copyright Secured   Used by Permission

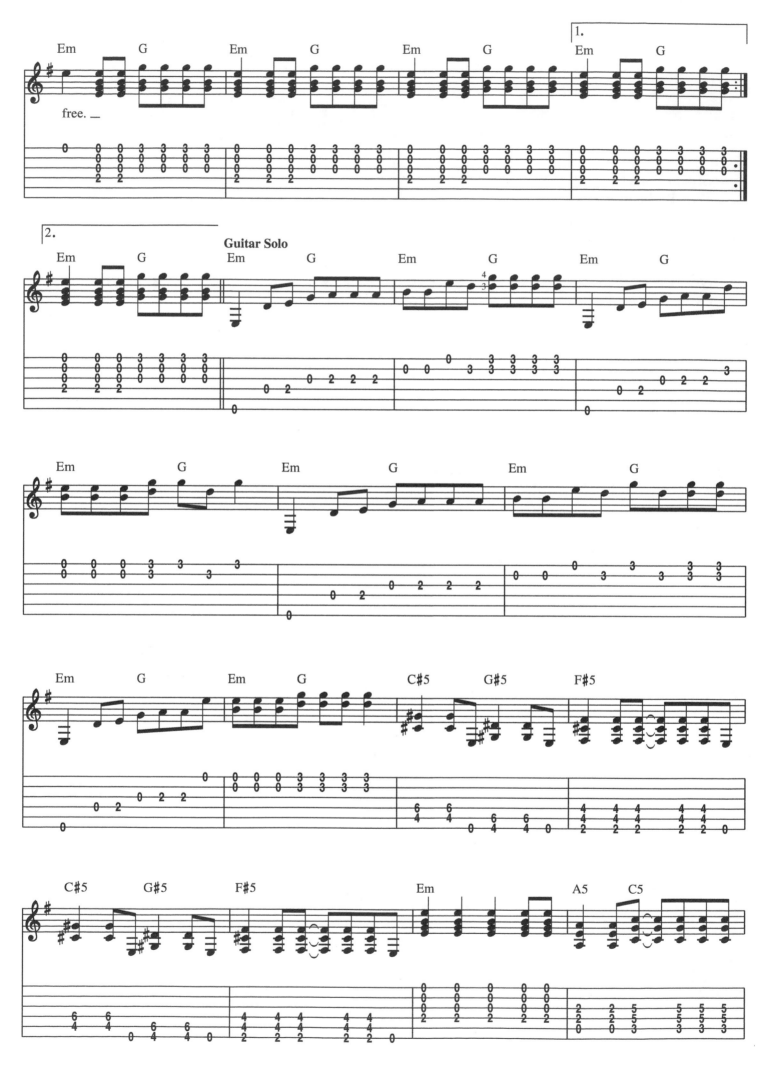

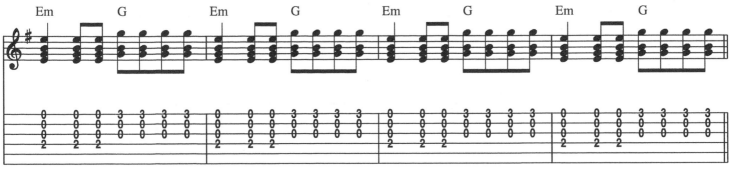

⊕ Coda

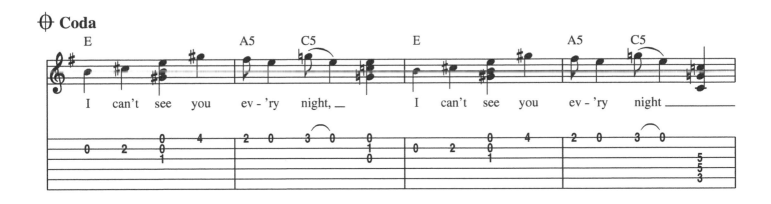

*Use Pattern 10

Outro

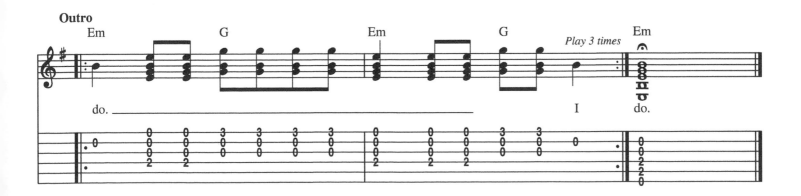

Additional Lyrics

2. I'm standing in your line,
   I do, hope you have the time.
   I do, pick a number to,
   I do, keep a date with you.

Across the Universe

Words and Music by John Lennon and Paul McCartney

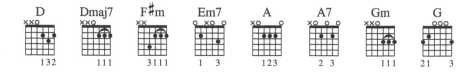

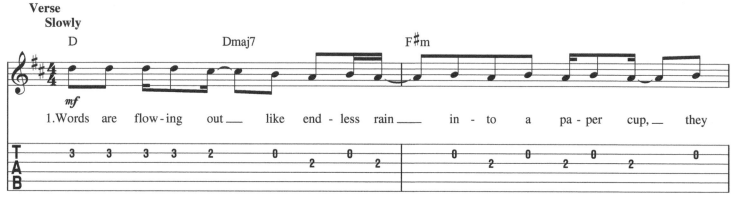

*Combine Patterns 9 & 10 for $\frac{5}{4}$ meas.
*Use Pattern 10 for $\frac{2}{4}$ meas.

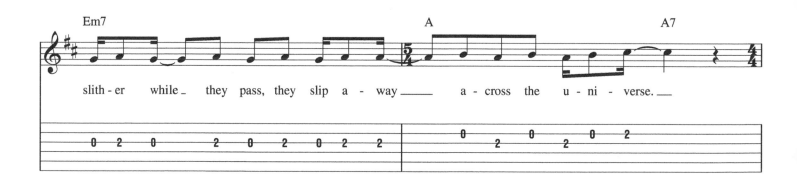

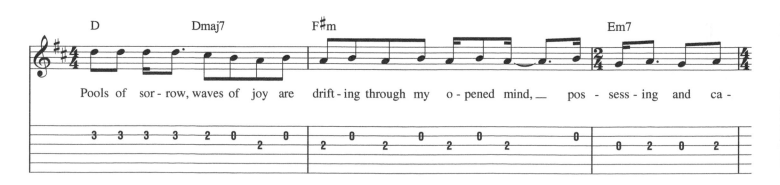

Copyright © 1968, 1970 Sony/ATV Music Publishing LLC
Copyright Renewed
All Rights Administered by Sony/ATV Music Publishing LLC, 8 Music Square West, Nashville, TN 37203
International Copyright Secured All Rights Reserved

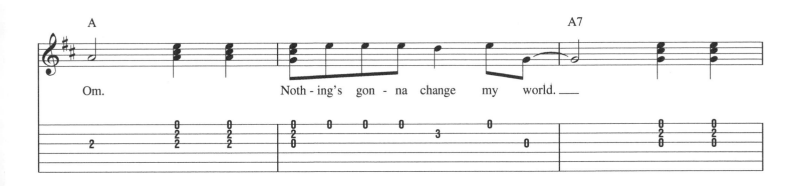

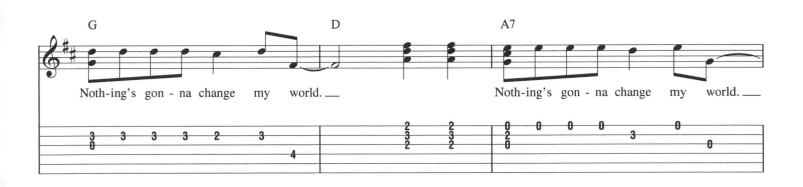

eyes, they call me on and on ___ a - cross ___ the u - ni - verse. ___

Thoughts me - an - der like a rest - less wind in - side a let - ter box, ___ they

D.S. al Coda

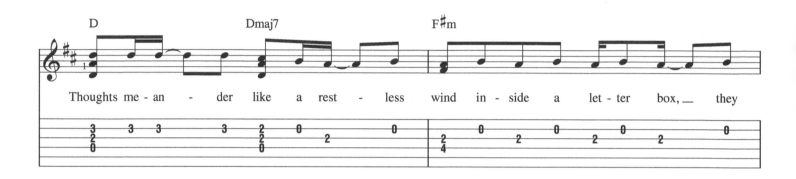

tum - ble blind - ly as they make their way a - cross ___ the u - ni - verse. ___

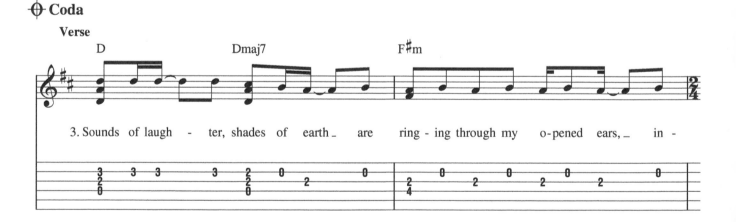

⊕ **Coda**

Verse

3. Sounds of laugh - ter, shades of earth ___ are ring - ing through my o - pened ears, ___ in -

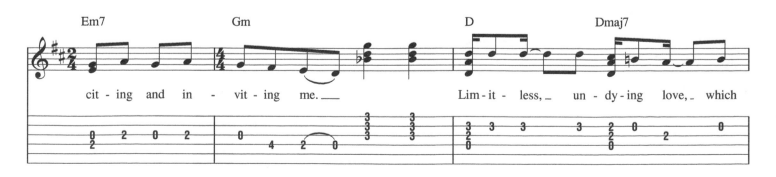

cit - ing and in - vit - ing me. ___ Lim - it - less, ___ un - dy - ing love, ___ which

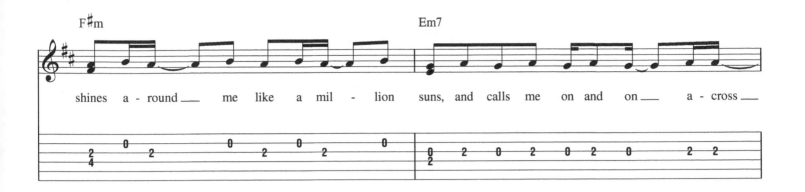

American Pie

Words and Music by Don McLean

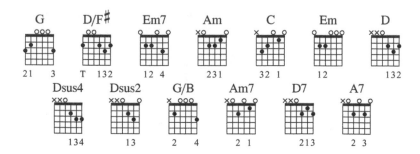

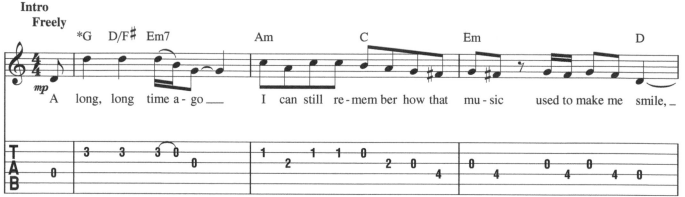

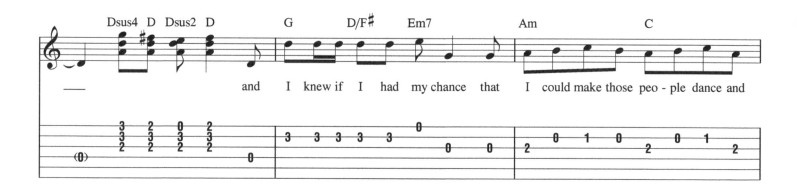

*One strum per chord throughout Intro

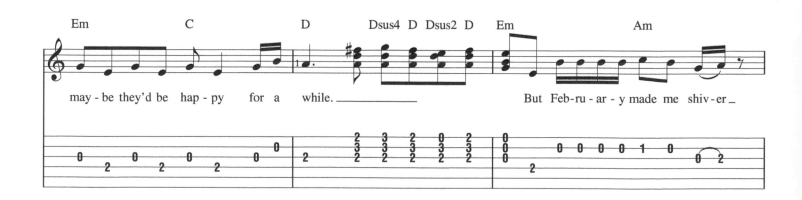

Copyright © 1971, 1972 BENNY BIRD CO., INC.
Copyright Renewed
All Rights Controlled and Administered by SONGS OF UNIVERSAL, INC.
All Rights Reserved   Used by Permission

with ev - 'ry pa - per I'd de - liv - er. Bad news on the door - step, I could-n't take one more step. I

can't re - mem - ber if I cried when I read a - bout his wid - owed bride,

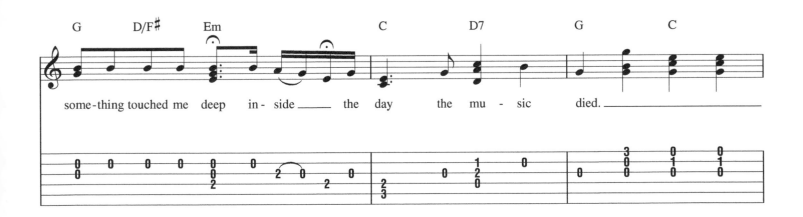

some - thing touched me deep in - side _____ the day the mu - sic died. _____

Strum Pattern: 2
Pick pattern: 2
Chorus
*Moderately

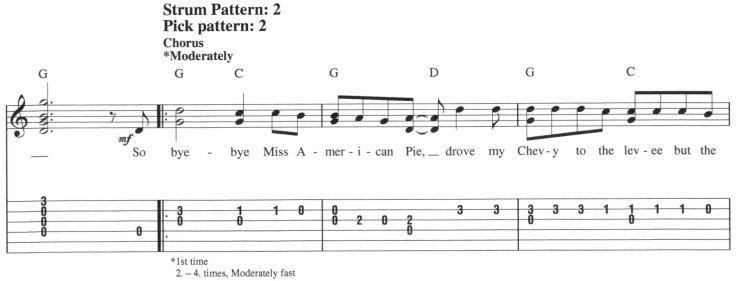

_____ So bye - bye Miss A - mer - i - can Pie, ___ drove my Chev - y to the lev - ee but the

*1st time
2. – 4. times, Moderately fast

lev - ee was dry. ___ Them good ole boys were drink - in' whis - key and rye, ___ sing - in'

Strum Pattern: 1
Pick Pattern: 2

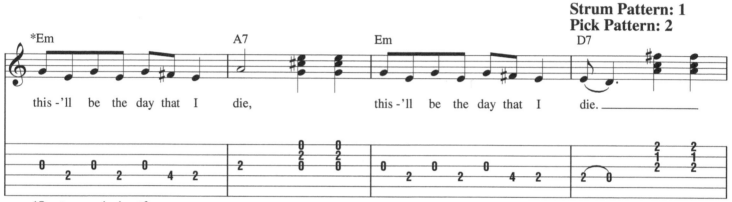

this -'ll be the day that I die, this -'ll be the day that I die. ___

*One strum per chord next 3 meas.

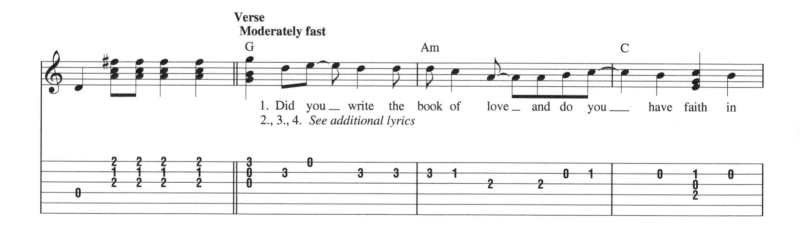

Verse
Moderately fast

1. Did you ___ write the book of love ___ and do you ___ have faith in
2., 3., 4. *See additional lyrics*

God a - bove ___ if the Bi - ble tells ___ you so? ___ Now do

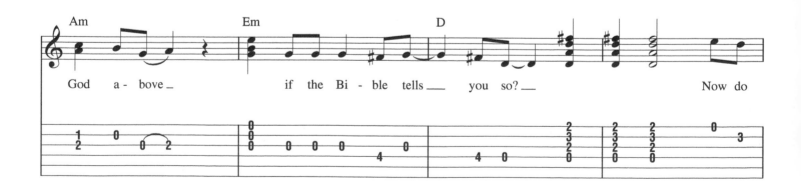

you be - lieve __ in rock and roll, __ can mu - sic save your mor - tal soul, __ and

can you teach me how to dance __ real slow? _____ Well, I

know that you're in love with him __ 'cause I saw you danc - in' in the gym. __ You

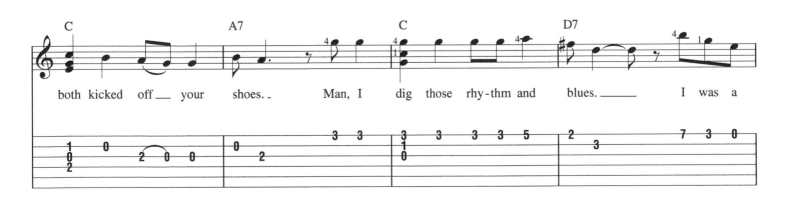

both kicked off __ your shoes. __ Man, I dig those rhy - thm and blues. _____ I was a

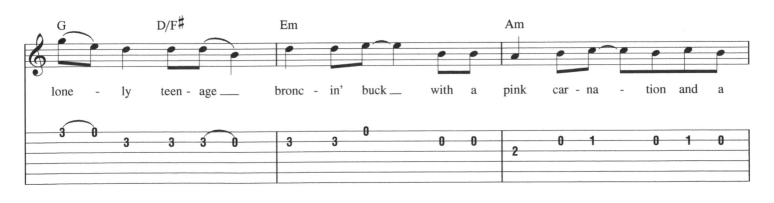

lone - ly teen - age ___ bronc - in' buck __ with a pink car - na - tion and a

13

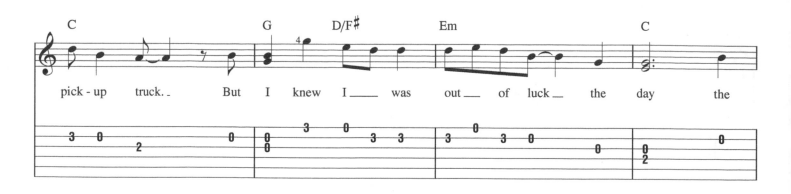

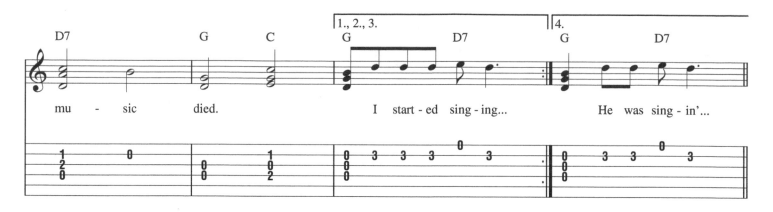

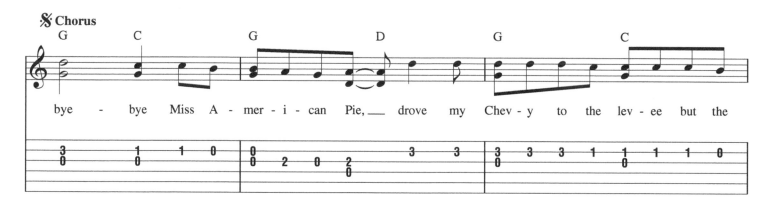

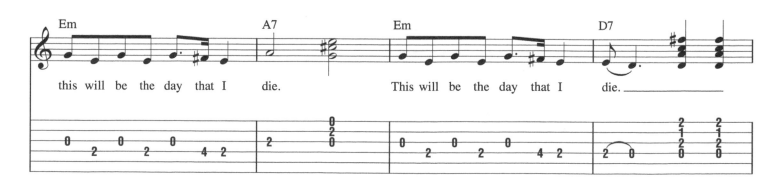

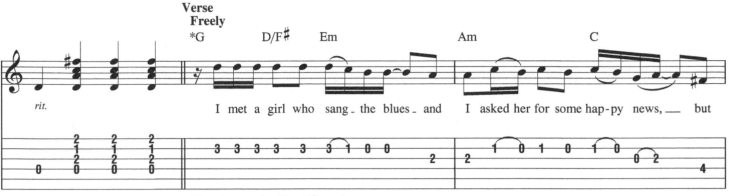

Verse
Freely

*One strum per chord (next 18 meas.)

I met a girl who sang the blues and I asked her for some hap-py news, but

she just smiled and turned a - way. I went down to the sa-cred store where I

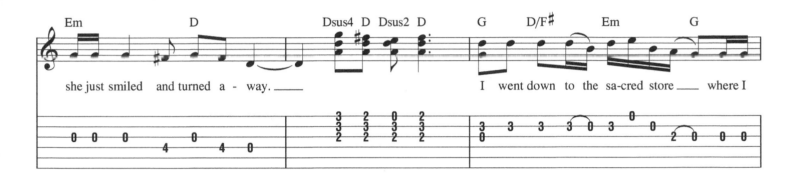

heard the mu - sic years be-fore, but the man there said the mu - sic would-n't play. And

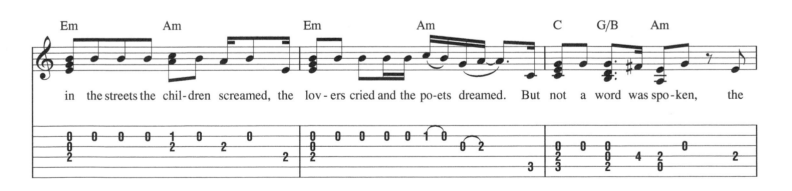

in the streets the chil-dren screamed, the lov - ers cried and the po-ets dreamed. But not a word was spo-ken, the

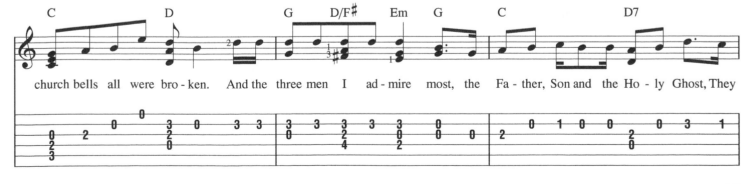

church bells all were bro - ken. And the three men I ad - mire most, the Fa - ther, Son and the Ho - ly Ghost, They

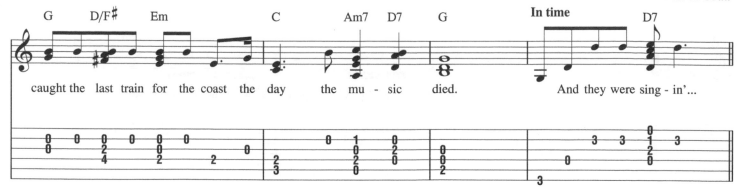

caught the last train for the coast the day the mu - sic died. And they were sing - in'...

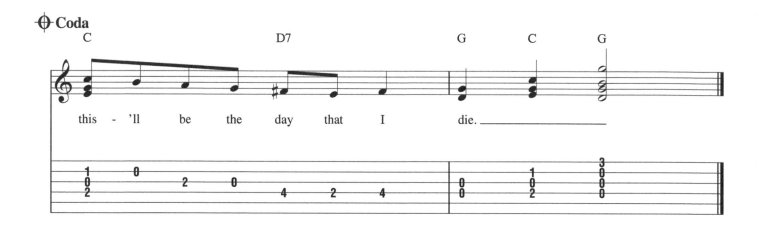

this - 'll be the day that I die. _____

Additional Lyrics

2. Now for ten years we've been on our own, and moss grows fat on a rollin' stone.
But, that's not how it used to be.
When the jester sang for the king and queen in a coat he borrowed from James Dean.
And a voice that came from you and me.
Oh, and while the king was looking down, the jester stole his thorny crown.
The courtroom was adjourned, no verdict was returned.
And while Lenin read a book on Marx, a quartet practiced in the park.
And we sang dirges in the dark, the day the music died.
We were singin'...

3. Helter-skelter in the summer swelter, the birds flew off with a fallout shelter,
Eight miles high and fallin' fast.
It landed foul on the grass. The players tried for a forward pass,
With the jester on the sidelines in a cast.
Now, the half-time air was sweet perfume, while the sergeants played a marching tune.
We all got up to dance, oh, but we never got the chance.
'Cause the players tried to take the field, the marching band refused to yield.
Do you recall what was revealed the day the music died?
We started singin'...

4. Oh, and there we were all in one place, a generation lost in space,
With no time left to start again.
So, come on, Jack be nimble, Jack be quick. Jack Flash sat on a candlestick,
'Cause fire is the devil's only friend.
Oh, and as I watched him on the stage my hands were clenched in fists of rage.
No angel born in hell could break that Satan's spell.
And as the flames climbed high into the night to light the sacrificial rite,
I saw Satan laughing with delight, the day the music died.
He was singin'...

Maggie May

Words and Music by Rod Stewart and Martin Quittenton

Strum Pattern: 2, 3
Pick Pattern: 2, 4

Intro
Moderately

1. Wake up, Mag - gie, I think I got some-thing to say to you.
morn - ing sun, when it's in your face real - ly shows your age.
3. All I need - ed was a friend __ to lend a guid - ing hand.
4. *See additional lyrics*

It's late Sep - tem - ber and I real - ly should be,
But that don't wor - ry me none. In my eyes you're
But you turned in - to a lov - er, and moth - er what a lov - er! You

back at __ school.
ev - er - y - thing.
wore me __ out.

I know I keep you a -
I laughed at all of your
All you did was wreck my

Copyright © 1971 by Unichappell Music Inc., Rod Stewart and EMI Full Keel Music
Copyright Renewed 1999
All Rights for Rod Stewart Controlled and Administered by EMI Blackwood Music Inc.
International Copyright Secured   All Rights Reserved

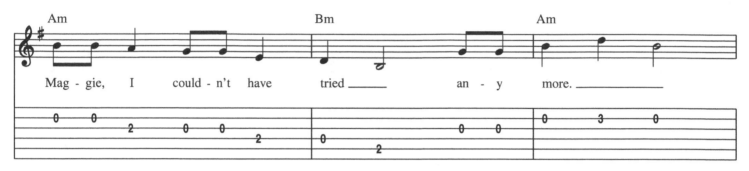

Chorus

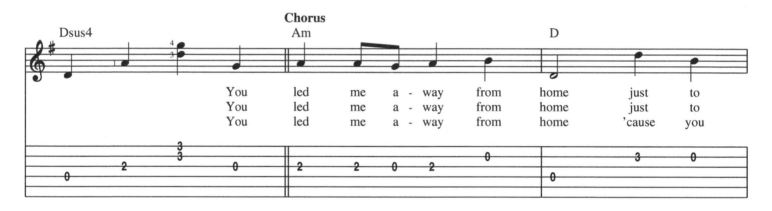

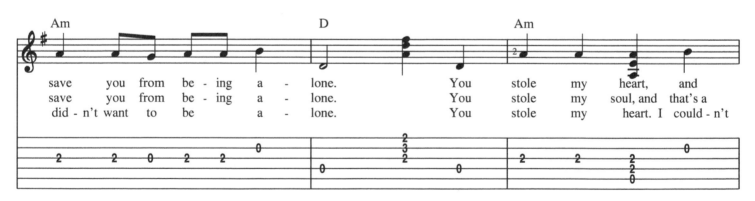

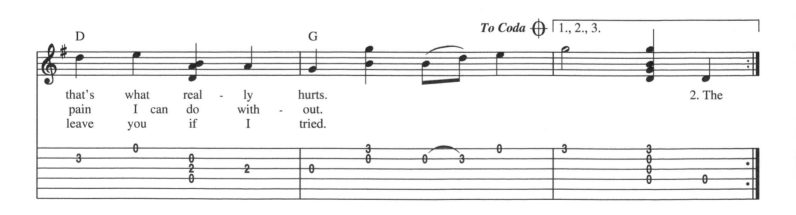

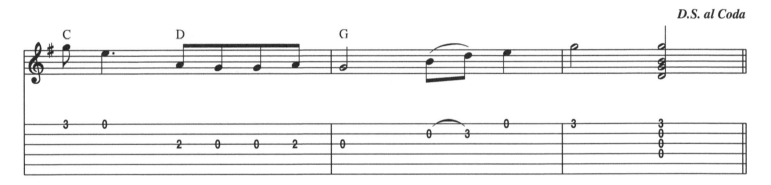

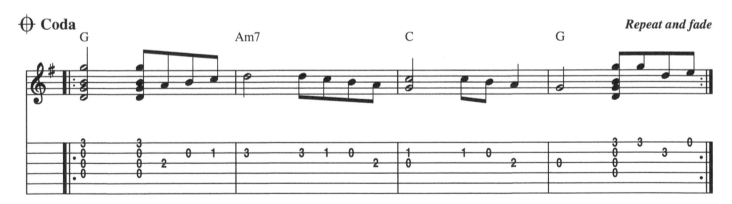

Additional Lyrics

4. I suppose I could collect my books
   And get on back to school.
   Or steal my daddy's cue
   And make a living out of playing pool.
   Or find myself a rock 'n' roll band
   That needs a helping hand.
   Oh, Maggie, I wish I'd never seen your face.
   You made a first class fool out of me.
   But I'm as blind as a fool can be.
   You stole my heart, but I love you anyway.

Blowin' in the Wind

Words and Music by Bob Dylan

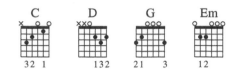

Strum Pattern: 2
Pick Pattern: 3, 2

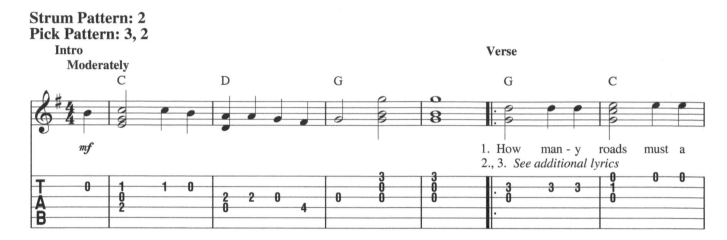

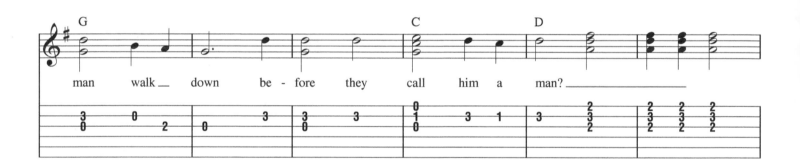

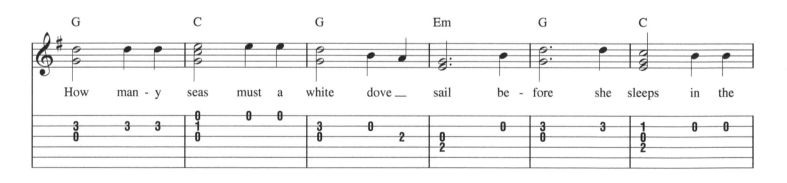

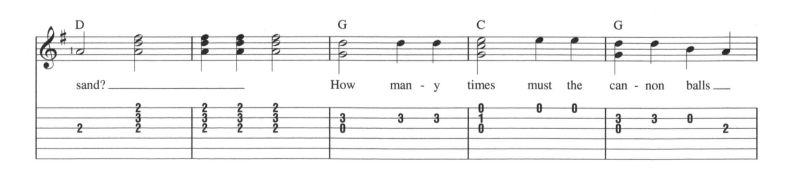

Copyright © 1962 Warner Bros. Inc.
Copyright Renewed 1990 Special Rider Music
International Copyright Secured   All Rights Reserved
Reprinted by Permission of Music Sales Corporation

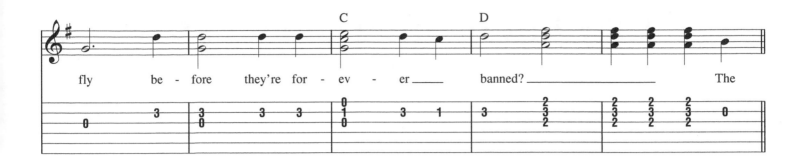

fly   be - fore   they're   for - ev - er ___ banned? _____ The

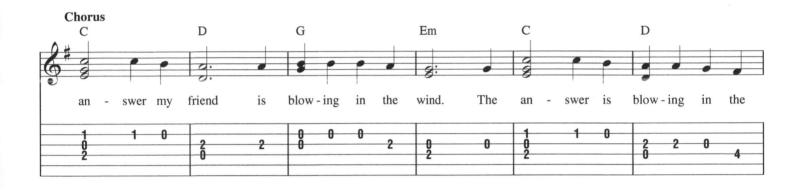

Chorus

an - swer   my   friend   is   blow-ing   in   the   wind.   The   an - swer   is   blow-ing   in   the

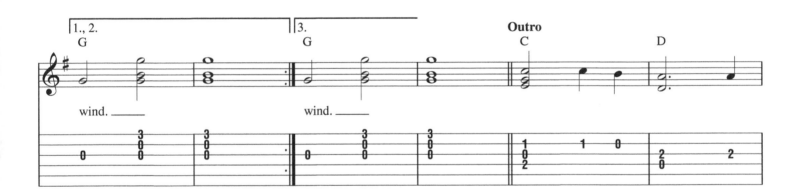

1., 2. | 3. | **Outro**

wind. ___   wind. ___

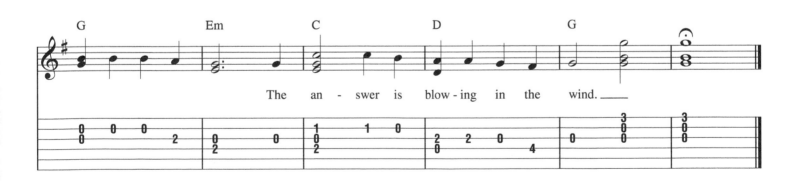

The   an - swer   is   blow-ing   in   the   wind. ___

Additional Lyrics

2. How many years must a mountain exist
Before it is washed to the sea?
How many years can some people exist
Before they're allowed to be free?
How many times can a man turn his head
And pretend that he just doesn't see?

3. How many times must a man look up
Before he can see the sky?
How many ears must one man have
Before he can hear people cry?
How many deaths will it take till he knows
That too many people have died?

Crazy Little Thing Called Love

Words and Music by Freddie Mercury

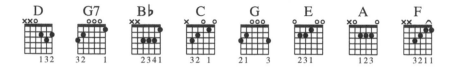

Strum Pattern: 1
Pick Pattern: 3

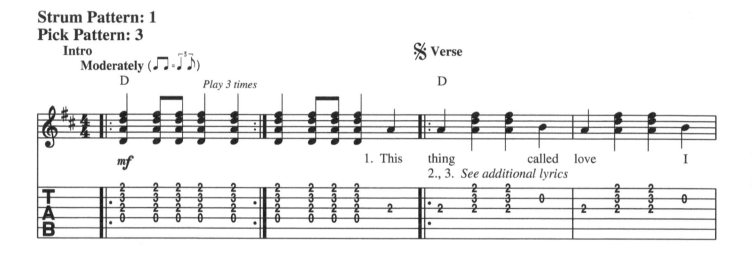

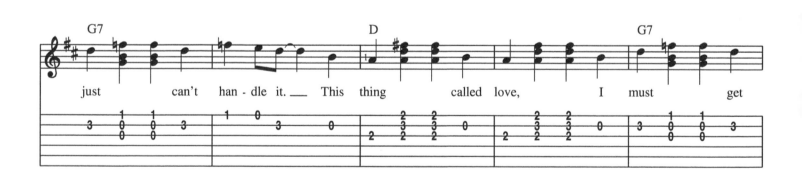

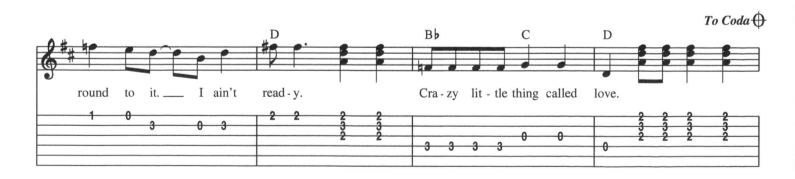

© 1979 QUEEN MUSIC LTD.
All Rights for the U.S. and Canada Controlled and Administered by BEECHWOOD MUSIC CORP.
All Rights for the world excluding the U.S. and Canada Controlled and Administered by EMI MUSIC PUBLISHING LTD.
All Rights Reserved   International Copyright Secured   Used by Permission

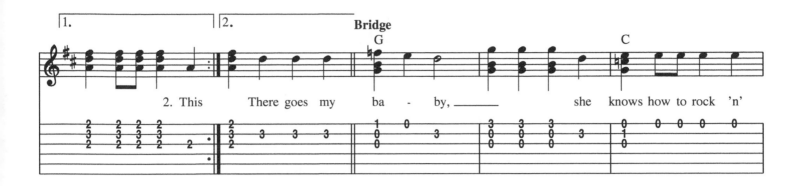

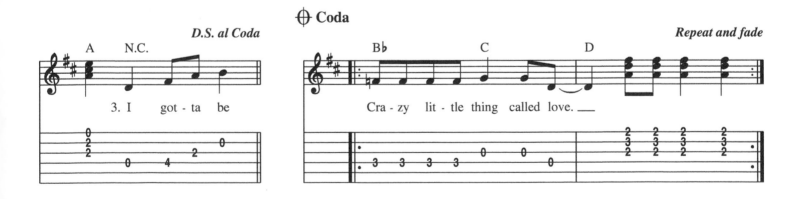

Additional Lyrics

2. This thing called love,
   It cries (like a baby) in a cradle all night.
   It swings, it jives,
   It shakes all over like a jellyfish.
   I kinda' like it.
   Crazy little thing called love.

3. I gotta be cool, relax,
   Get hip, get on my tracks.
   Take a backseat, hitchhike,
   And take a long ride on my motor bike
   Until I'm ready.
   Crazy little thing called love.

Free Bird

Words and Music by Allen Collins and Ronnie Van Zant

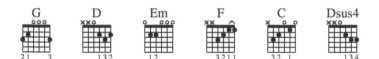

Strum Pattern: 1
Pick Pattern: 4

Intro
Slow Rock

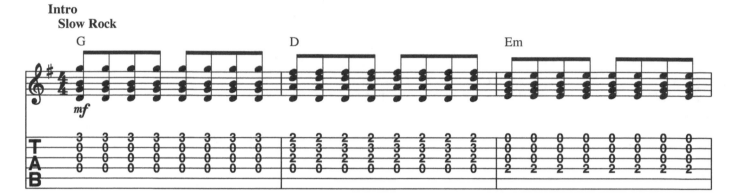

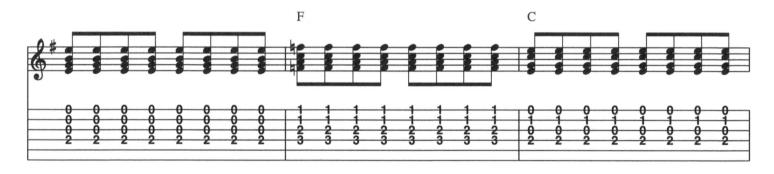

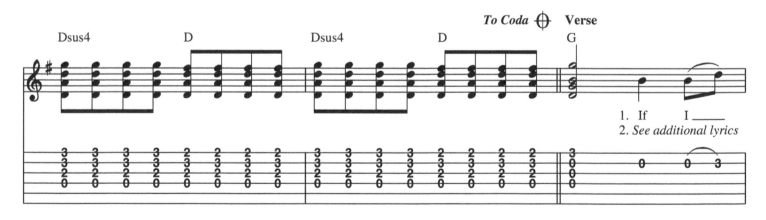

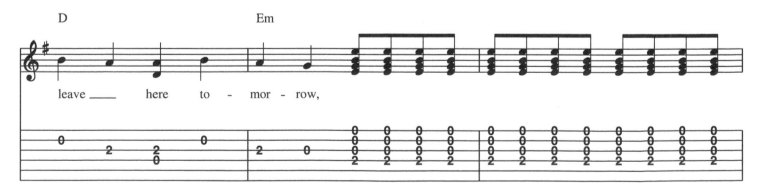

Copyright © 1973, 1975 SONGS OF UNIVERSAL, INC.
Copyrights Renewed
All Rights Reserved   Used by Permission

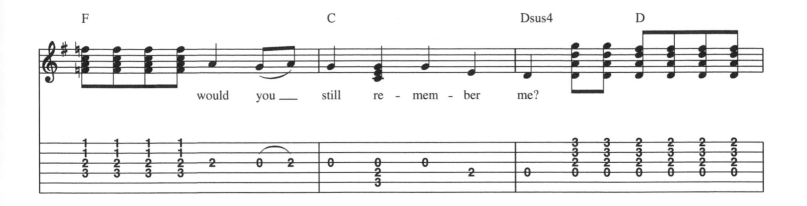

would you ___ still re - mem - ber me?

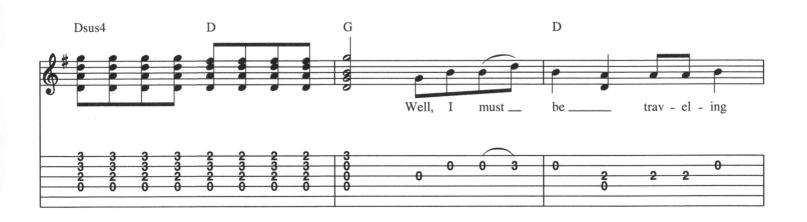

Well, I must ___ be ___ trav - el - ing

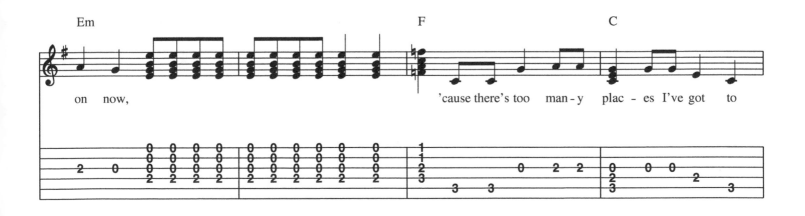

on now,   'cause there's too man - y plac - es I've got to

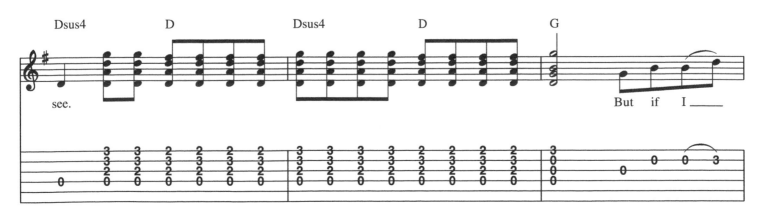

see.   But if I ___

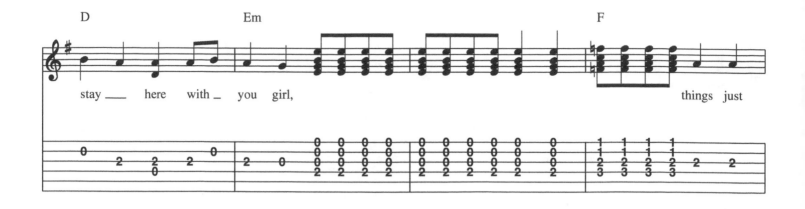

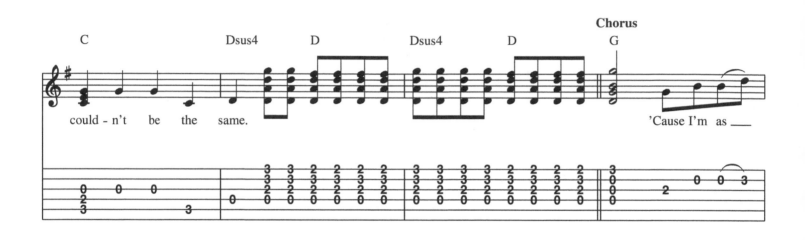

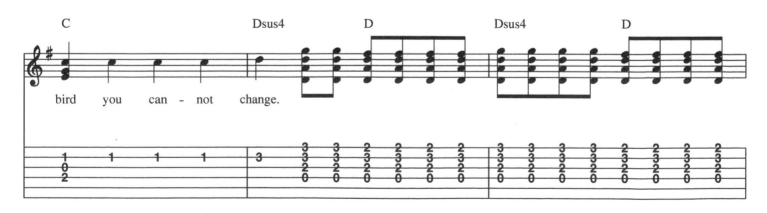

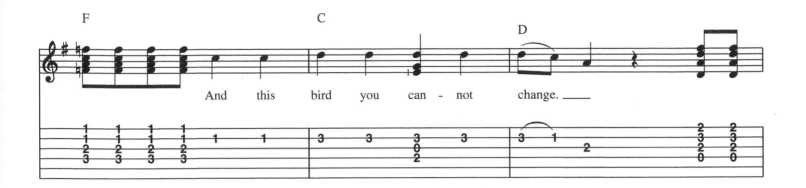

And this bird you can - not change. _____

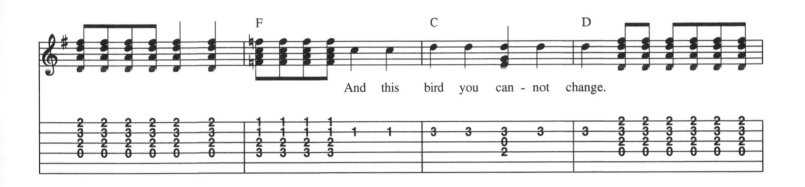

And this bird you can - not change.

Lord _____ knows, I can't _ change.

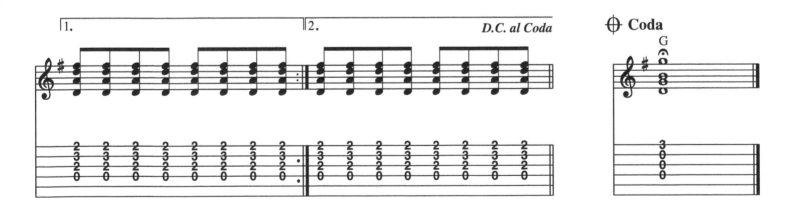

1.

2.

D.C. al Coda

⊕ **Coda**

Additonal Lyrics

2. Bye, bye baby, it's been sweet now, yeah, yeah,
   Though this feelin' I can't change.
   A please don't take it so badly,
   'Cause the Lord knows I'm to blame.
   But if I stay here with you girl,
   Things just couldn't be the same.

The Joker

Words and Music by Steve Miller, Eddie Curtis and Ahmet Ertegun

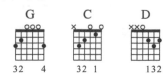

Strum Pattern: 3
Pick Pattern: 2

Copyright © 1973 by Sailor Music and Warner-Tamerlane Publishing Corp.
Copyright Renewed
All Rights Reserved   Used by Permission

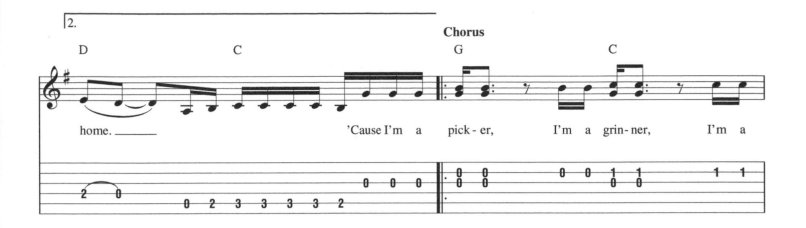

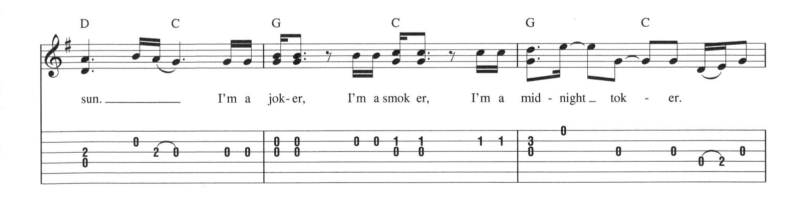

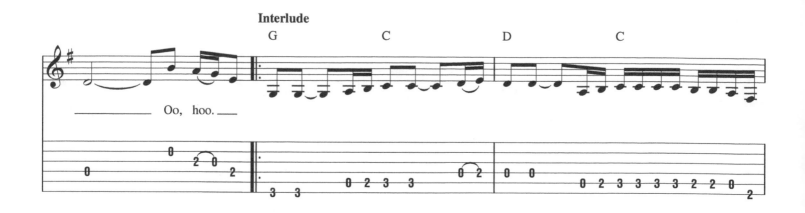

Interlude

Oo, hoo.

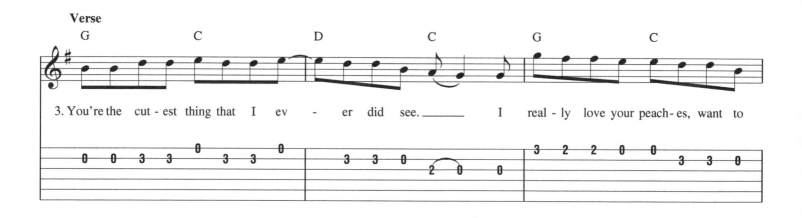

Verse

3. You're the cut - est thing that I ev - er did see._____ I real - ly love your peach - es, want to

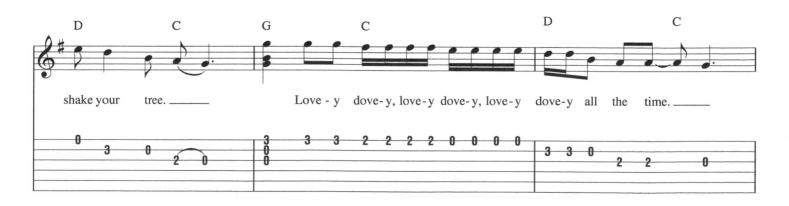

shake your tree._____ Love - y dove - y, love - y dove - y, love - y dove - y all the time._____

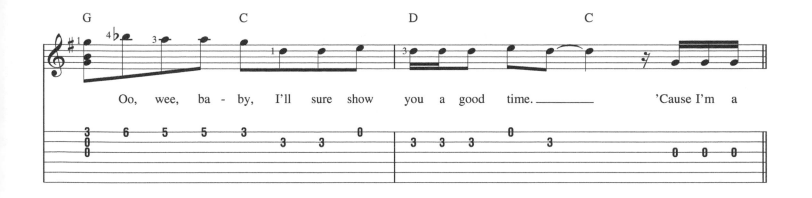

Oo, wee, ba - by, I'll sure show you a good time._____ 'Cause I'm a

Outro-Chorus

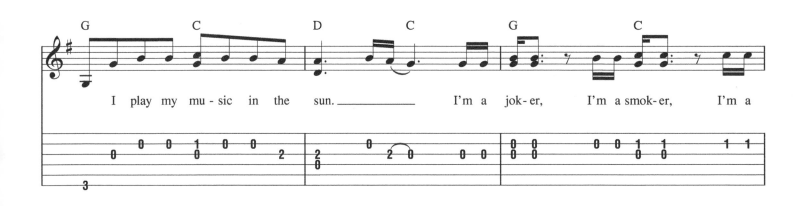

pick - er, I'm a grin - ner, I'm a lov - er, and I'm a sin - ner.

I play my mu - sic in the sun._____ I'm a jok-er, I'm a smok-er, I'm a

Repeat and fade

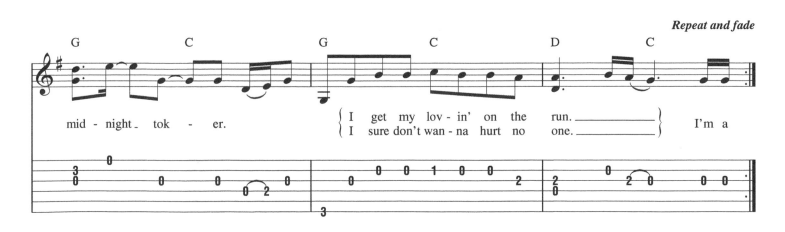

mid - night _ tok - er.

{ I get my lov - in' on the run._____
{ I sure don't wan - na hurt no one._____ }

I'm a

Landslide

Words and Music by Stevie Nicks

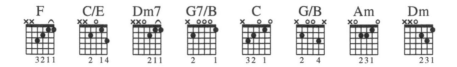

Strum Pattern: 1
Pick Pattern: 2

Intro
Moderately

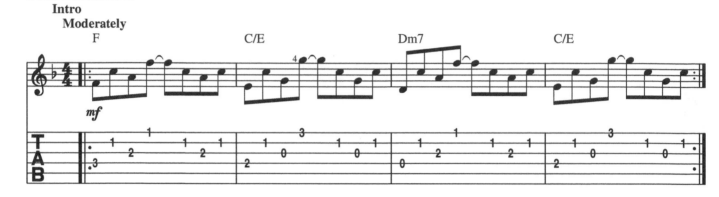

Verse

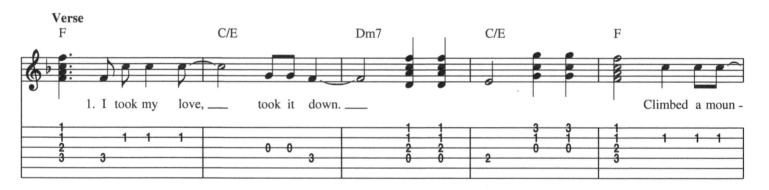

1. I took my love, ___ took it down. ___   Climbed a moun-

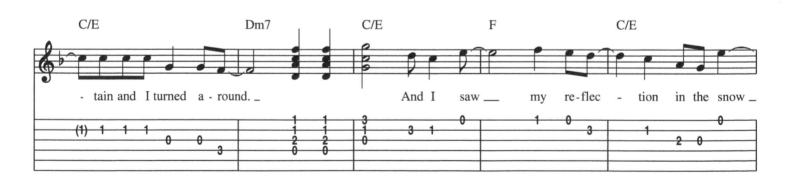

-tain and I turned a-round. _   And I saw ___ my re-flec - tion in the snow

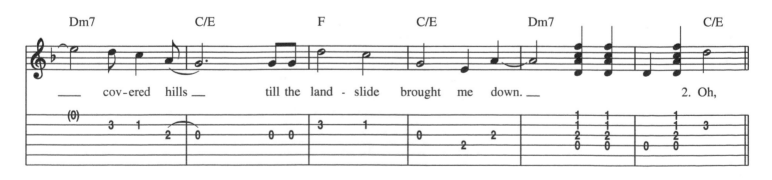

___ cov-ered hills ___   till the land - slide brought me down. ___   2. Oh,

Copyright © 1975 Welsh Witch Music
Copyright Renewed
All Rights Administered by Sony/ATV Music Publishing LLC, 8 Music Square West, Nashville, TN 37203
International Copyright Secured   All Rights Reserved

Verse

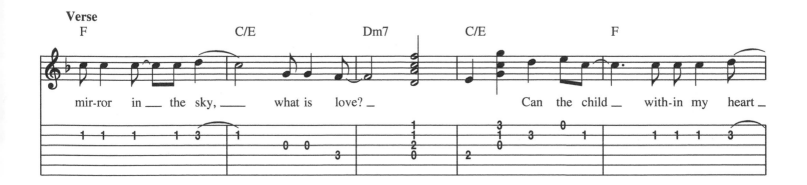

mir-ror in ___ the sky, ___ what is love? ___ Can the child ___ with-in my heart ___

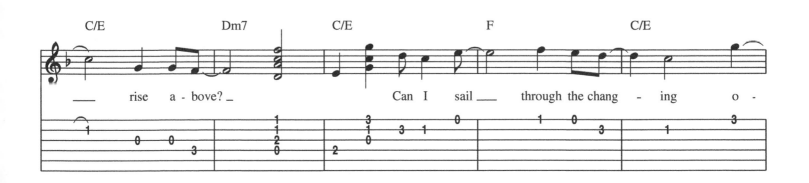

___ rise a - bove? ___ Can I sail ___ through the chang – ing o -

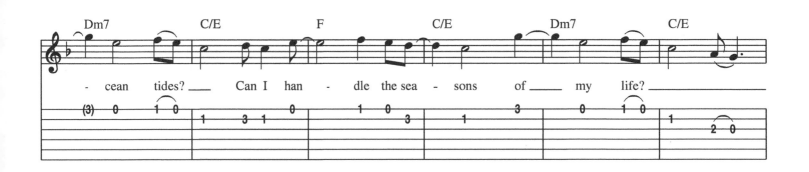

- cean tides? ___ Can I han - dle the sea - sons of ___ my life? ___

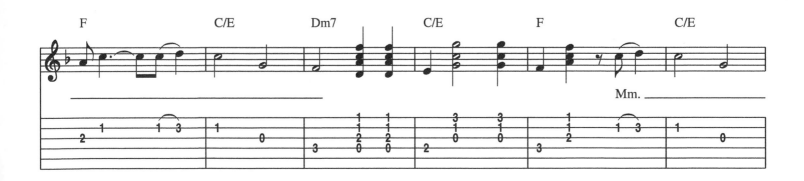

Mm. ___

𝄋 Chorus

Well, I've ___ been ___ a-fraid ___ of chang - ing 'cause I've built ___

— my life ____ a - round ____ you. ____ But time ____ makes ____ you bold -

-er; e-ven child-ren ____ get old-er, and I'm ____ get-tin' old-er, too. ____

Interlude

D.S. al Coda

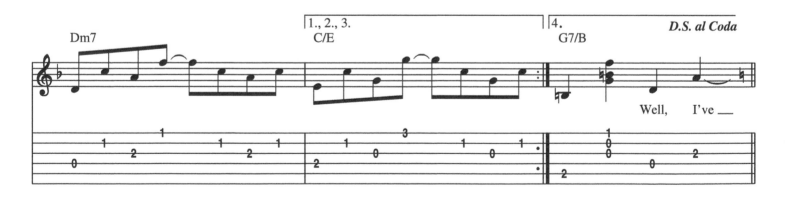

Well, I've ____

Coda

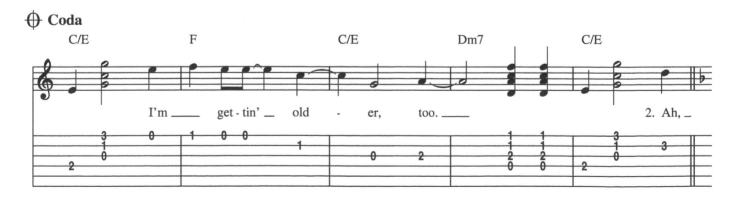

I'm ____ get-tin' ____ old-er, too. ____ 2. Ah, __

Verse

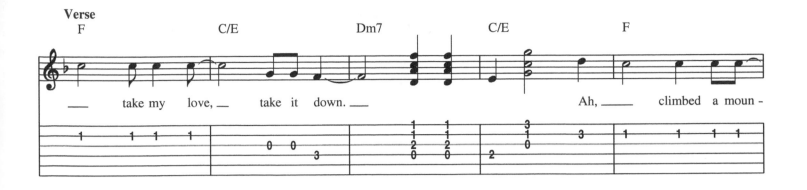

take my love, __ take it down. __ Ah, __ climbed a moun-

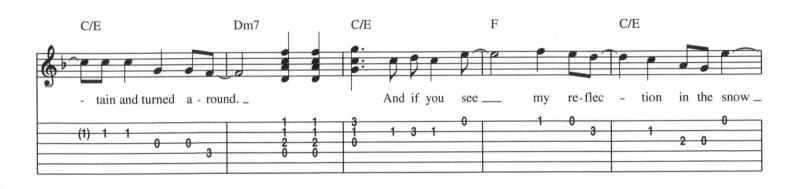

-tain and turned a-round. _ And if you see __ my re-flec - tion in the snow __

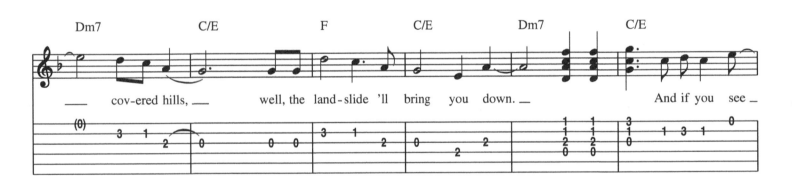

__ cov-ered hills, __ well, the land-slide 'll bring you down. _ And if you see _

__ my re-flec - tion in the snow __ cov-ered hills, _____ well, the land - slide 'll

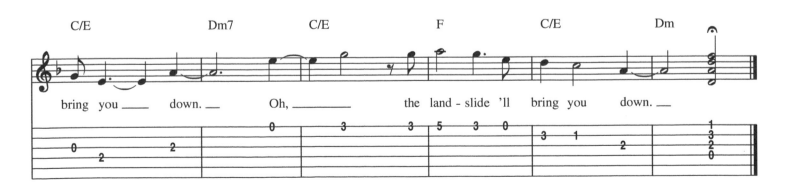

bring you __ down. _ Oh, _____ the land - slide 'll bring you down. _

Layla

Words and Music by Eric Clapton and Jim Gordon

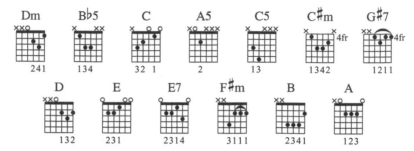

Strum Pattern: 3
Pick Pattern: 3

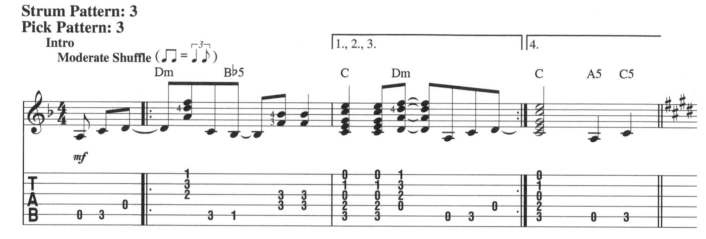

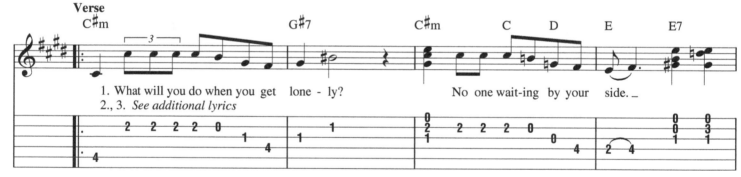

Copyright © 1970 by Eric Patrick Clapton and Throat Music Ltd.
Copyright Renewed
All Rights for the U.S. Administered by Unichappell Music Inc.
International Copyright Secured   All Rights Reserved

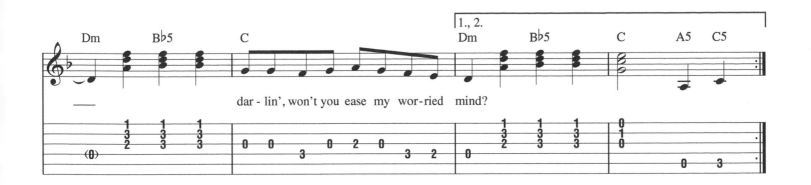

Additional Lyrics

2. Tried to give you consolation,
   Your old man had let you down.
   Like a fool, I fell in love with you.
   You turned my whole world upside down.

3. Make the best of the situation,
   Before I finally go insane.
   Please don't say we'll never find a way.
   Tell me all my love's in vain.

Midnight Rider

Words and Music by Gregg Allman and Robert Kim Payne

Strum Pattern: 3, 6
Pick Pattern: 2

Additional Lyrics

2. And I don't own the clothes I'm wearin'.
   And the road goes on forever.
   And I've got one more silver dollar.

3. And I'm gone past the point of carin'.
   Some ol' bed I'll soon be sharin',
   And I've got one more silver dollar.

Copyright © 1970 by Unichappell Music Inc. and Elijah Blue Music
Copyright Renewed
International Copyright Secured All Rights Reserved

One Headlight

Words and Music by Jakob Dylan

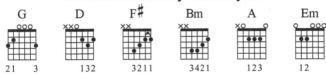

Strum Pattern: 2, 3
Pick Pattern: 3, 4

Intro
Moderately

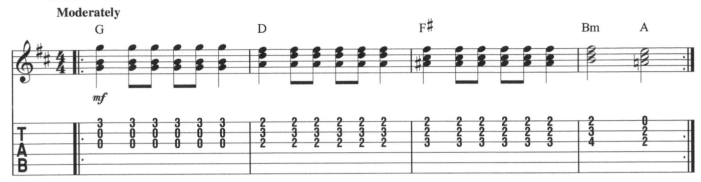

Verse

1. So long a-go, I don't re-mem-ber when, __ that's when they say I lost my on-ly
2. *See additional lyrics*

friend. __ Well, they said she died eas-y of a bro-ken-heart dis-ease, as I

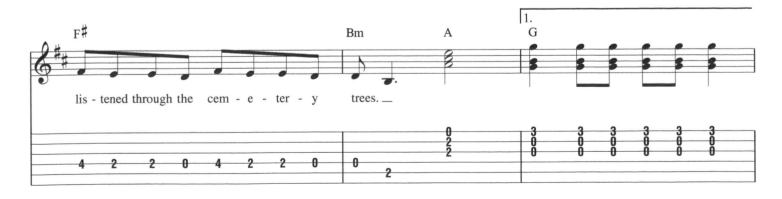

lis-tened through the cem-e-ter-y trees. __

Copyright © 1996 Brother Jumbo Music (ASCAP)
All Rights Administered by Wixen Music Publishing, Inc. as agent for Primary Wave Music Publishing, LLC
All Rights Reserved   Used by Permission

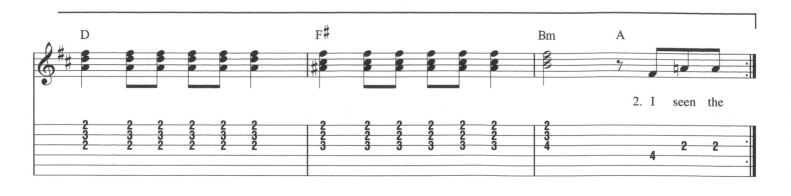

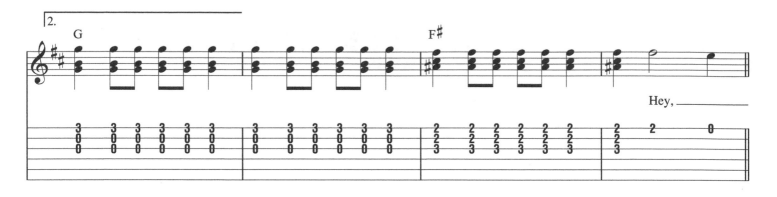

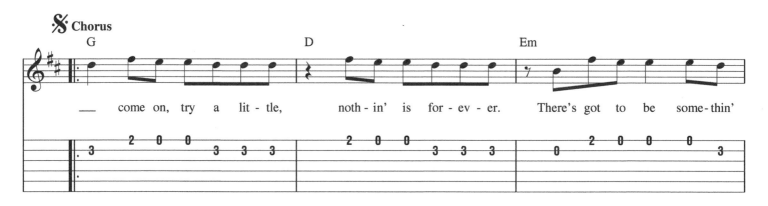

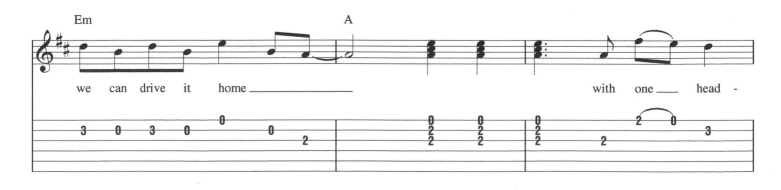

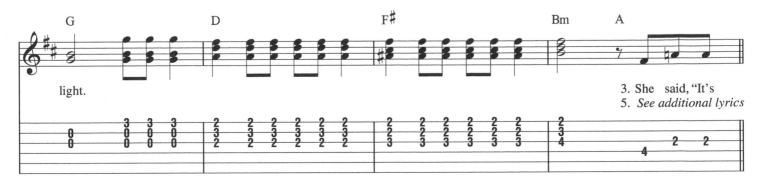

light.

3. She said, "It's
5. *See additional lyrics*

Verse

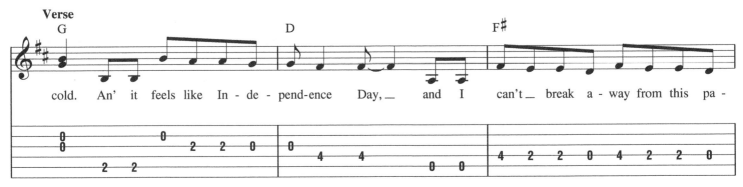

cold. An' it feels like In - de - pend-ence Day, __ and I can't __ break a - way from this pa -

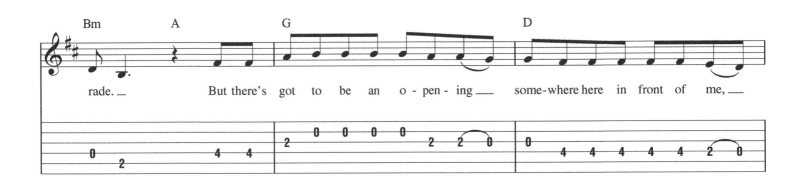

rade. __ But there's got to be an o - pen - ing __ some-where here in front of me, __

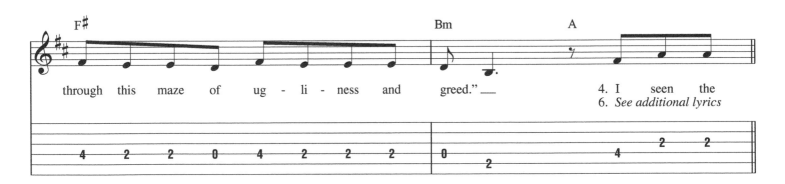

through this maze of ug - li - ness and greed." __

4. I seen the
6. *See additional lyrics*

Verse

sign __ up a - head __ at the Coun - ty Line Bridge, say - in,

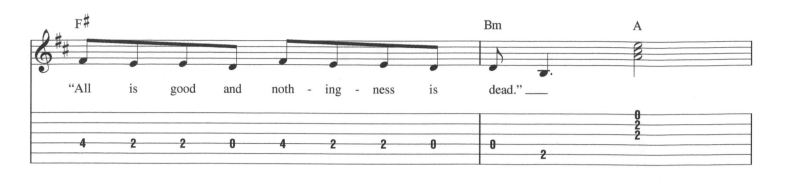

"All is good and noth - ing - ness is dead." ___

Run - ning till she's out of breath, she ran un - til there's noth - ing left. She

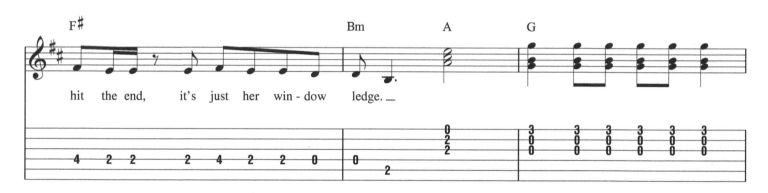

hit the end, it's just her win - dow ledge. ___

1.

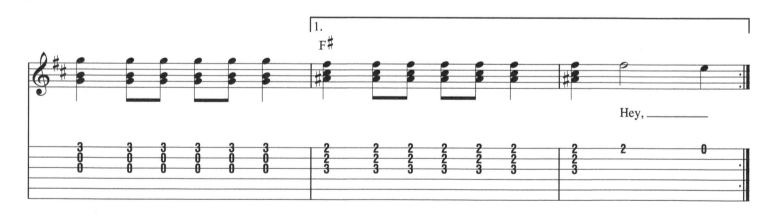

Hey, ___

2.

D.S. al Coda

Hey,   hey, ___   hey, ___

42

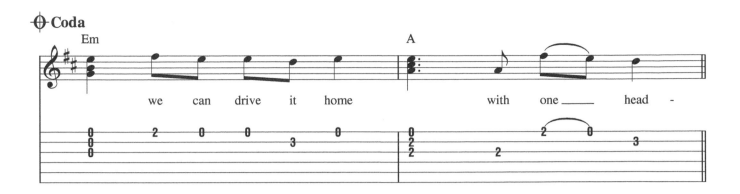

Outro

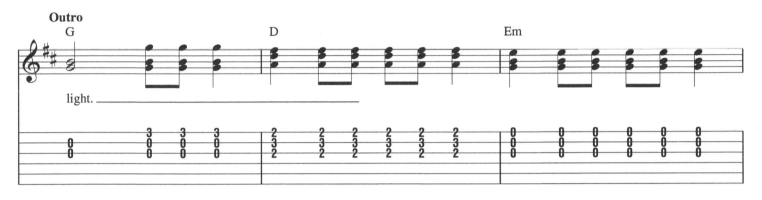

Repeat and fade

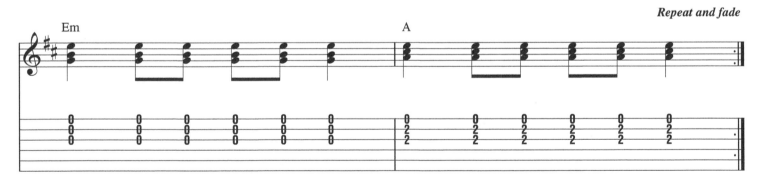

Additional Lyrics

2. I seen the sun comin' up at the funeral at dawn,
   Of the long broken arm of human law.
   Now, it always seemed such a waste,
   She always had a pretty face;
   I wondered why she hung around this place.

5. This place is old, and it feels just like a beat-up truck.
   I turn the engine, but the engine doesn't turn.
   It smells of cheap wine and cigarettes,
   This place is always such a mess;
   Sometimes I think I'd like to watch it burn.

6. Now I sit alone, and I feel just like somebody else.
   Man, I ain't changed, but I know I ain't the same.
   But somewhere here, in between these city walls of dying dreams,
   I think her death, it must be killing me.

Mrs. Robinson

Words and Music by Paul Simon

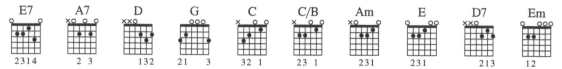

E7 A7 D G C C/B Am E D7 Em

*Capo II

Strum Pattern: 3, 5
Pick Pattern: 1, 3

Intro
Moderately fast

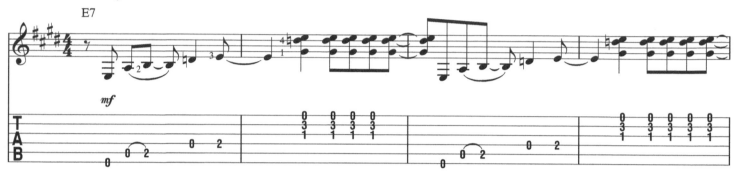

*Optional: To match recording, place capo at 2nd fret.

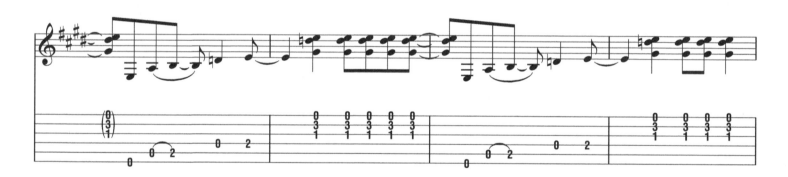

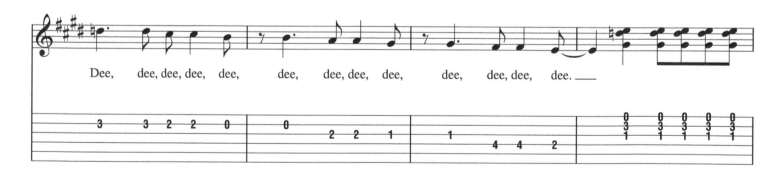

Dee, dee, dee, dee, dee, dee, dee, dee, dee, dee, dee, dee, dee. ___

Doo, doo, doo, doo, doo, doo, doo, doo, doo. ___

Copyright © 1968 (Renewed), 1970 (Renewed) Paul Simon (BMI)
International Copyright Secured   All Rights Reserved
Reprinted by Permission of Music Sales Corporation

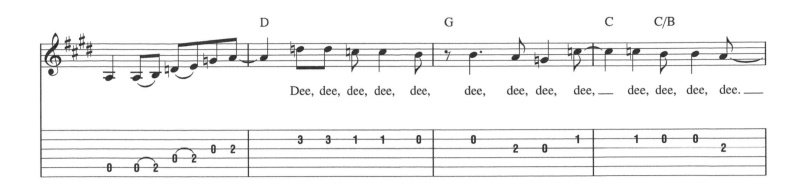

Dee, dee, dee, dee, dee, dee, dee, dee, dee, dee, dee, dee, dee.

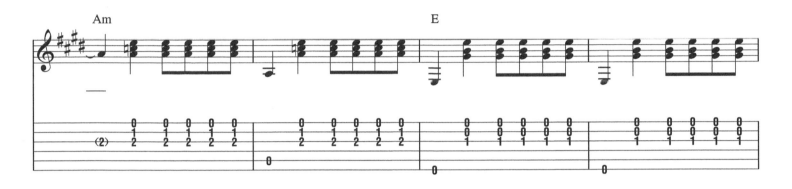

Chorus

1. And here's to you, _____ (3.) Miss-es Rob - in - son, _
4. *See additional lyrics*

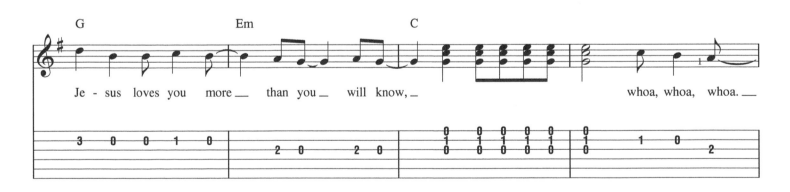

Je - sus loves you more __ than you __ will know, _ whoa, whoa, whoa. __

__ God bless you please, _ Miss-es Ro - bin - son. _

45

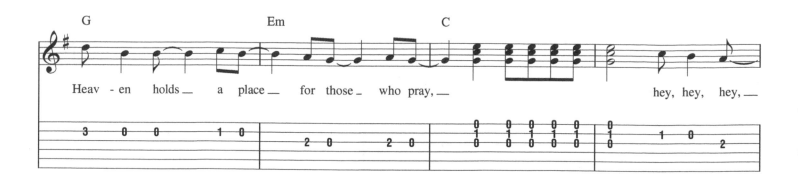

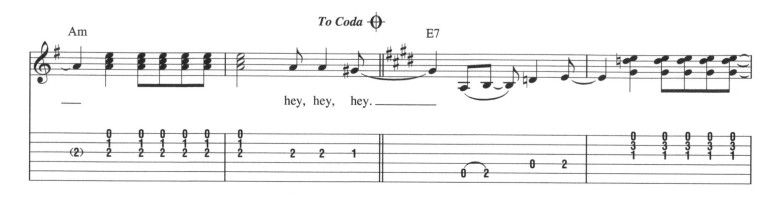

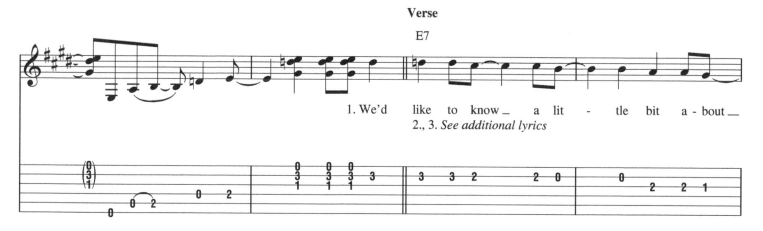

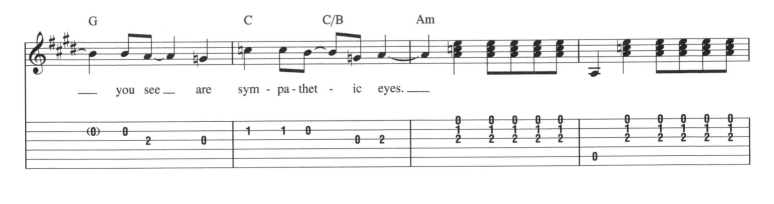

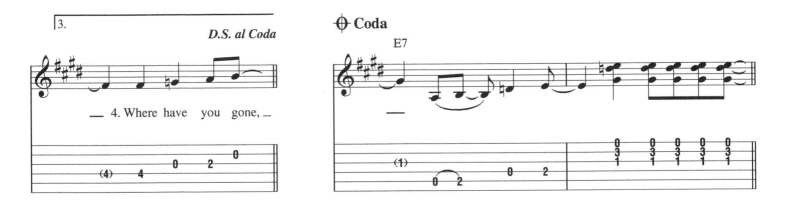

Outro

Repeat and fade

Additional Lyrics

2. Hide it in a hiding place where no one ever goes.
   Put in in your pantry with your cupcakes.
   It's a little secret, just the Robinsons' affair.
   Most of all you've got to hide it from the kids.

3. Sitting on a sofa on a Sunday afternoon.
   Going to the candidates debate.
   Laugh about it, shout about it when you've got to choose.
   Ev'ry way you look at this you lose.

Chorus 4. Where have you gone, Joe DiMaggio?
   A nation turns its lonely eyes to you, woo, woo, woo.
   What's that you say, Mrs. Robinson?
   Joltin' Joe has left and gone away,
   Hey, hey, hey, hey, hey, hey.

Name

Words and Music by John Rzeznik

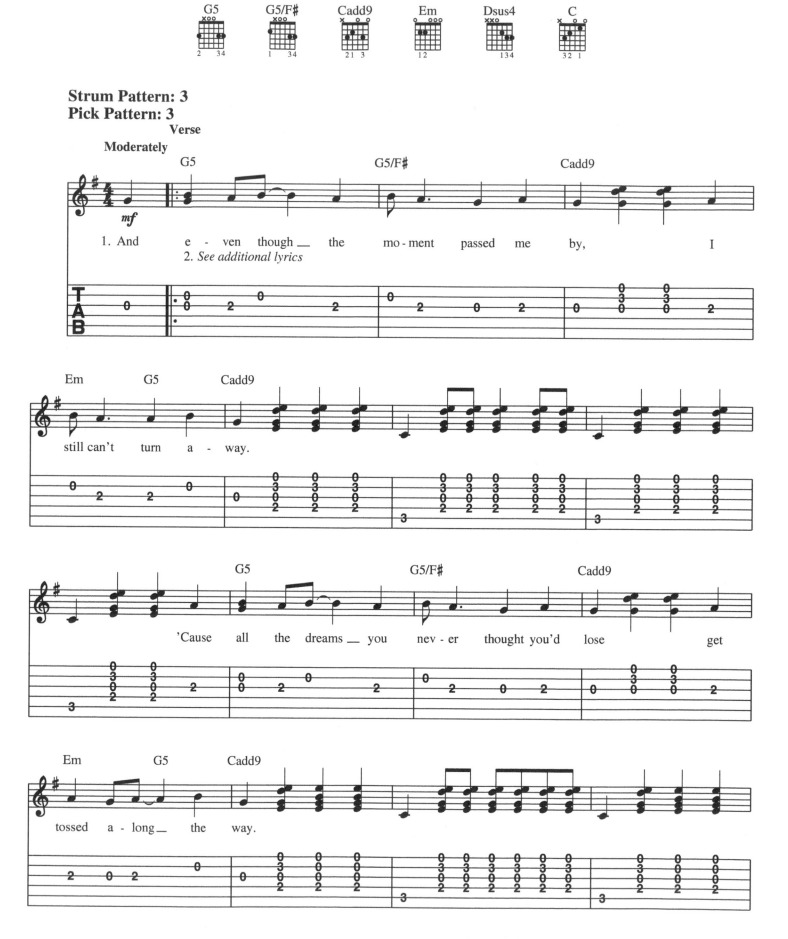

© 1995 EMI VIRGIN SONGS, INC., FULL VOLUME MUSIC and SCRAP METAL MUSIC
All Rights Controlled and Administered by EMI VIRGIN SONGS, INC. (BMI)
All Rights Reserved   International Copyright Secured   Used by Permission

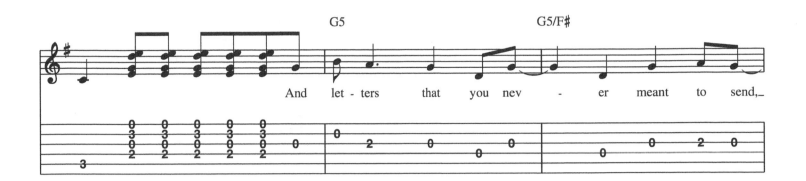

And let - ters that you nev - er meant to send,

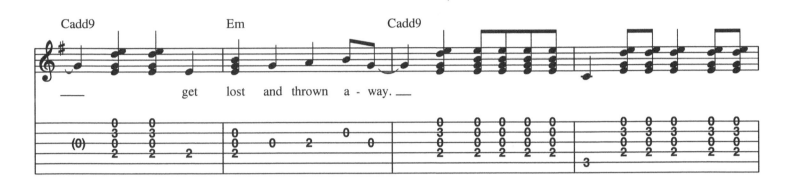

get lost and thrown a - way. ___

Chorus

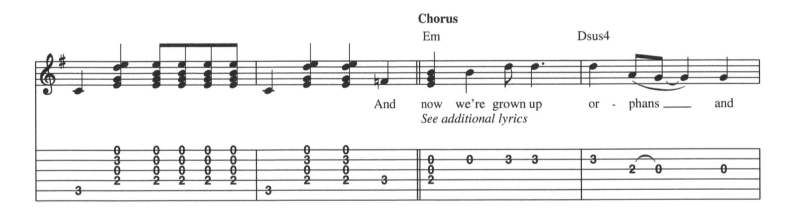

And now we're grown up or - phans ___ and
See additional lyrics

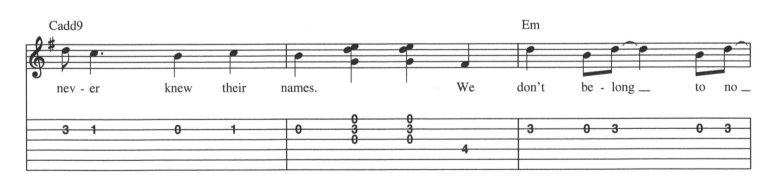

nev - er knew their names. We don't be - long ___ to no ___

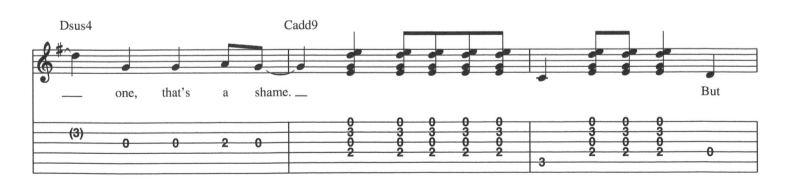

___ one, that's a shame. ___ But

Em   Dsus4   Cadd9

you could hide be side ___ me,   may - be   for   a - while.

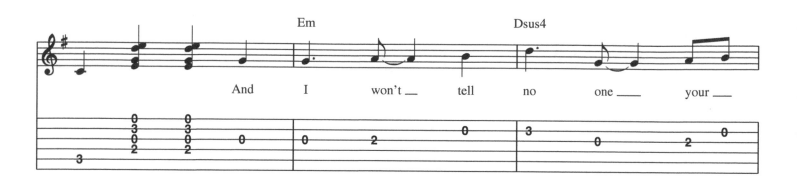

Em   Dsus4

And   I   won't __ tell   no   one __ your __

Cadd9

name.   And   I   won't tell 'em your

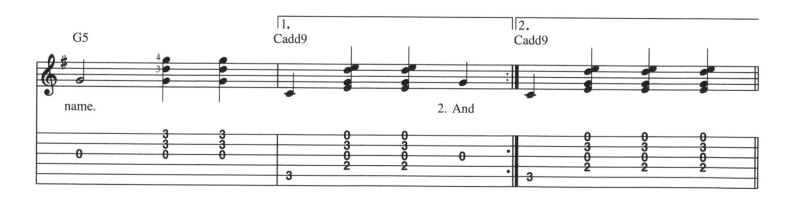

G5   1.   Cadd9   2.   Cadd9

name.   2. And

Verse

G5   G5/F#   Cadd9   Em   G5

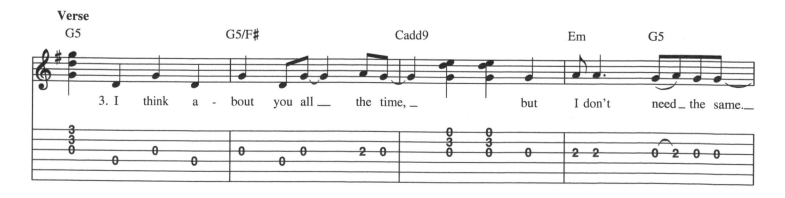

3. I think a - bout you all __ the time, _   but   I don't   need _ the same. _

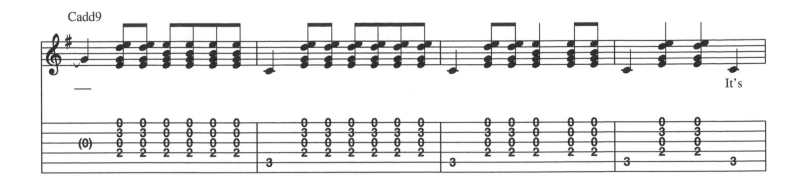

Additional Lyrics

2. And scars are souvenirs you never lose,
   The past is never far.
   And did you lose yourself somewhere out there,
   Did you get to be a star?
   And don't it make you sad to know that life
   Is more than who we are?

Chorus We grew up way too fast
   Now there's nothin' to believe
   When reruns all become our history.
   A tired song keeps playin' on a tired radio.
   And I won't tell no one your name.
   And I won't tell 'em your name.

Only Wanna Be with You

Words and Music by Darius Carlos Rucker, Everett Dean Felber, Mark William Bryan, and James George Sonefeld

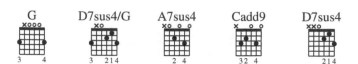

Strum Pattern: 4
Pick Pattern: 4

Verse
Moderately fast

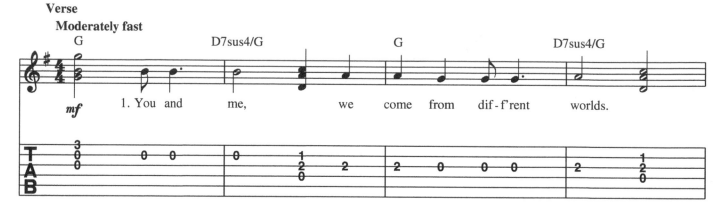

1. You and me, we come from dif-f'rent worlds.

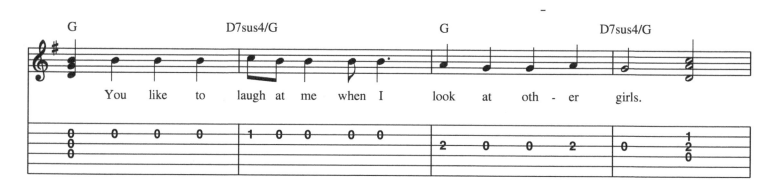

You like to laugh at me when I look at oth-er girls.

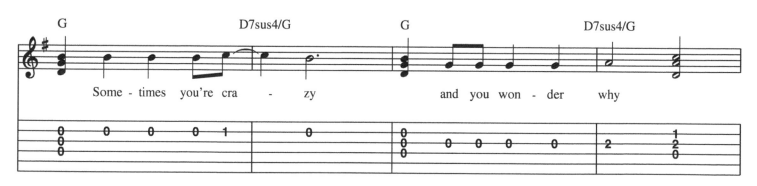

Some-times you're cra-zy and you won-der why

I'm such a ba-by 'cause the Dol-phins make me cry. Well, there's

© 1994 EMI APRIL MUSIC INC. and MONICA'S RELUCTANCE TO LOB
All Rights Controlled and Administered by EMI APRIL MUSIC INC.
All Rights Reserved   International Copyright Secured   Used by Permission

Chorus

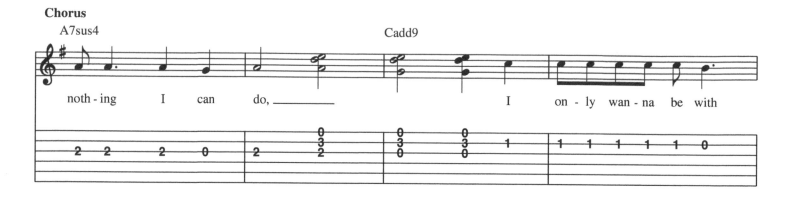

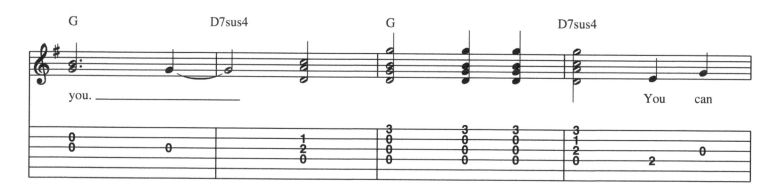

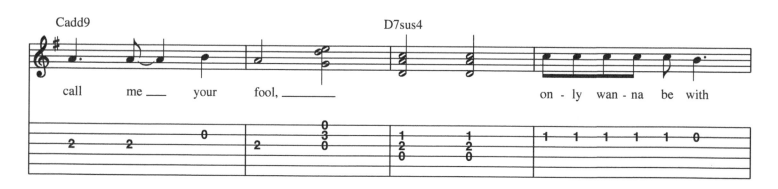

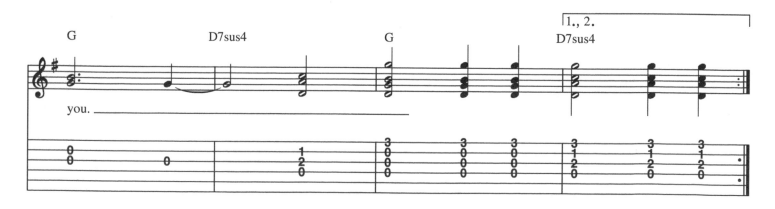

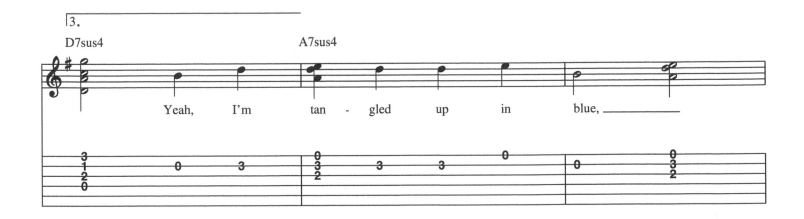

Yeah, I'm tan - gled up in blue, _____

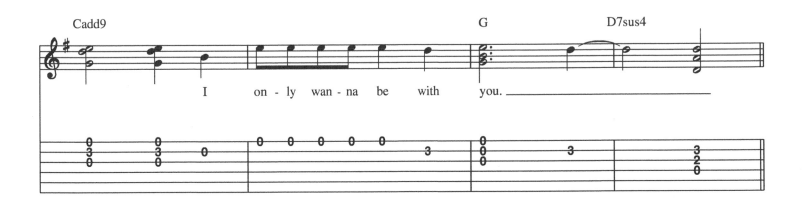

I on - ly wan - na be with you. _____

Outro   *Repeat and fade*

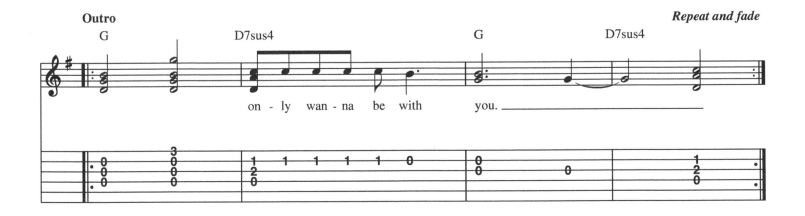

on - ly wan - na be with you. _____

Additional Lyrics

3. Put on a little Dylan, sitting on a fence.
   I say, "That line is great." You ask me what I meant by,
   "Said I shot a man named Gray, took his wife to Italy.
   She inherit a million bucks and when she died it came to me,
   I can't help it if I'm lucky." Only wanna be with you.
   Ain't Bobby so cool? Only wanna be with you.

4. Sometimes I wonder if it will ever end.
   You get so mad at me when I go out with my friends.
   Sometimes you're crazy and you wonder why
   I'm such a baby, yeah, the Dolphins make me cry.
   Well, there's nothing I can do, only wanna be with you.
   You can call me your fool, only wanna be with you.

Soak Up the Sun

Words and Music by Jeff Trott and Sheryl Crow

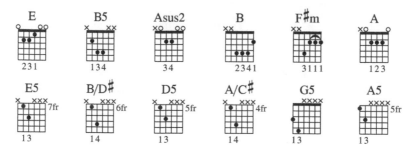

Strum Pattern: 3
Pick Pattern: 4

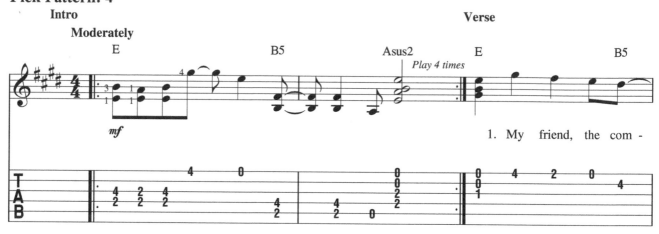

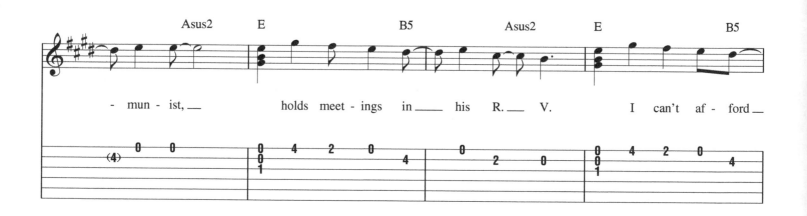

Copyright © 2001 by Cyrillic Soup, Warner-Tamerlane Publishing Corp. and Old Crow Music
All Rights Reserved   Used by Permission

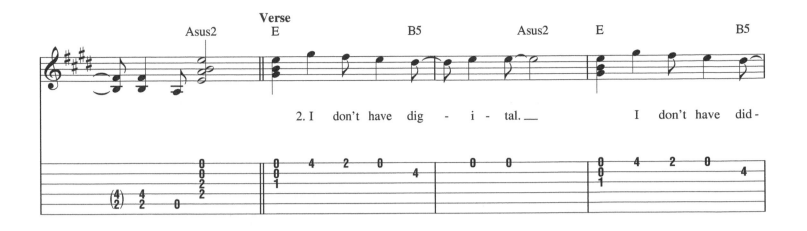

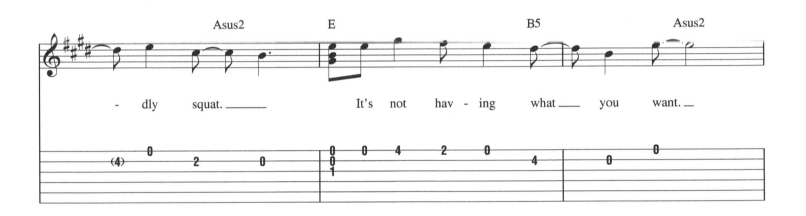

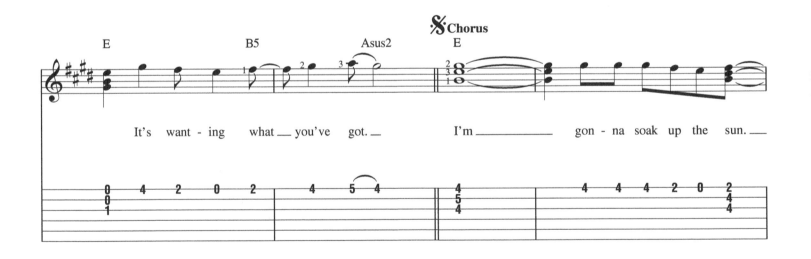

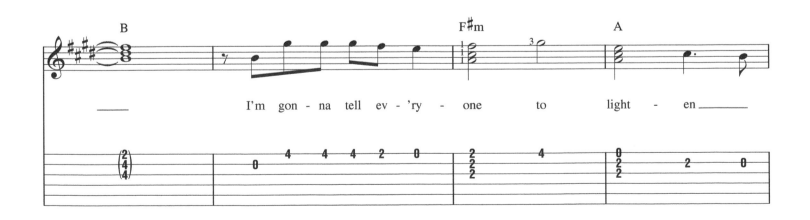

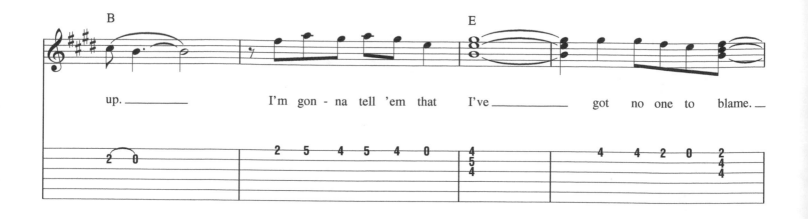

up. _____ I'm gon - na tell 'em that I've _____ got no one to blame. _____

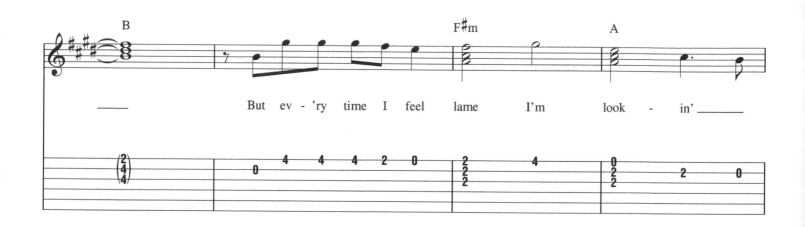

_____ But ev - 'ry time I feel lame I'm look - in' _____

To Coda 1 ⊕ **Interlude**

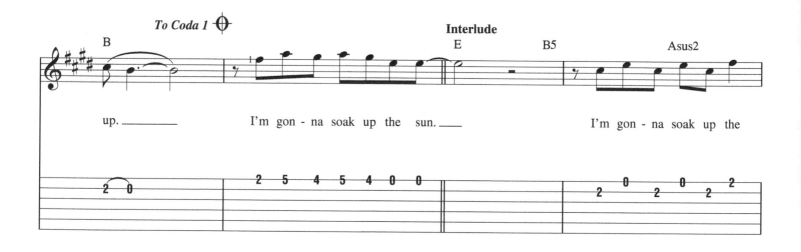

up. _____ I'm gon - na soak up the sun. _____ I'm gon - na soak up the

𝄋𝄋 **Verse**

sun. _____

3. I've got a crum - my job. _____
4. Don't have no mas - ter suite, _____

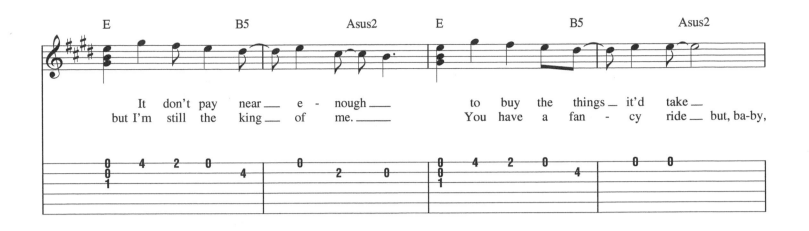

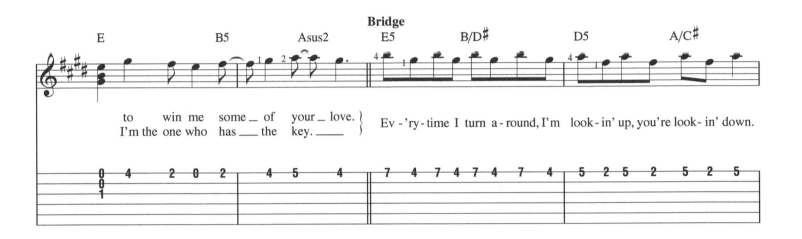

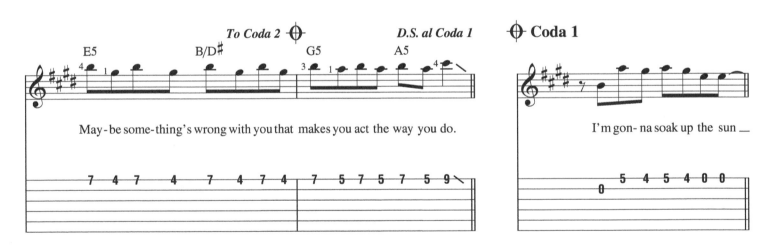

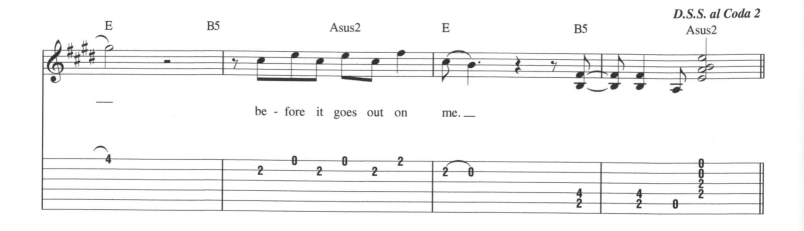

D.S.S. al Coda 2

be - fore it goes out on me. ___

Coda 2

makes you act the way you do. May - be I am cra - zy too.

Chorus

I'm ___ gon - na soak up the sun. ___ I'm gon - na tell ev - 'ry -

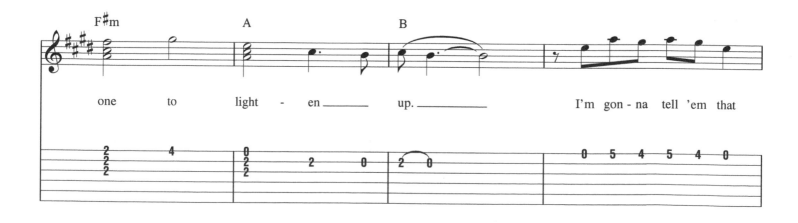

one to light - en ___ up. ___ I'm gon - na tell 'em that

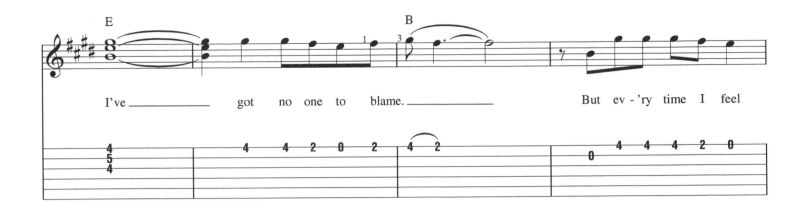

I've _____ got no one to blame. _____ But ev-'ry time I feel

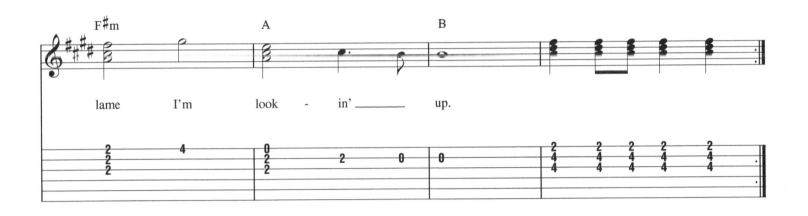

lame I'm look - in' _____ up.

Outro

I, _____ I'm gon - na soak up the sun. _____

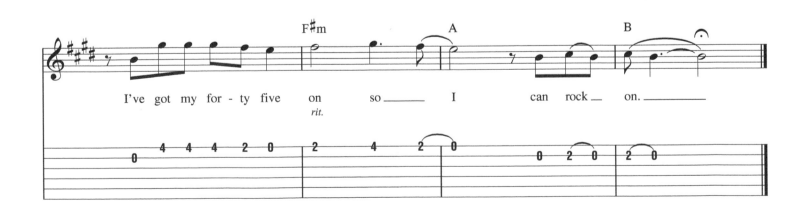

I've got my for - ty five on so _____ I can rock _____ on. _____

rit.

Somebody to Love

Words and Music by Darby Slick

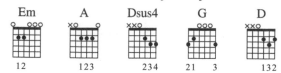

Strum Pattern: 5, 6
Pick Pattern: 1, 6

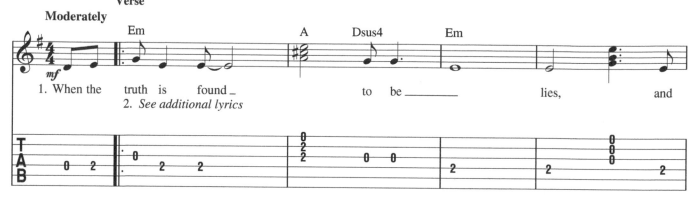

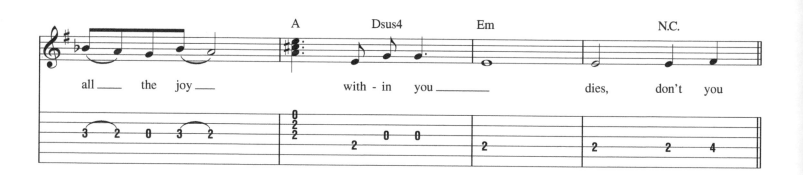

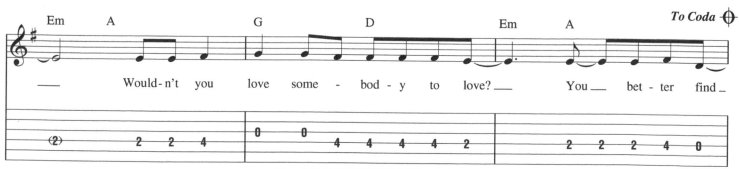

Copyright © 1967 IRVING MUSIC, INC.
Copyright Renewed
All Rights Reserved   Used by Permission

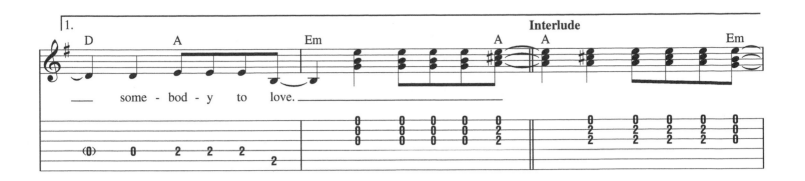

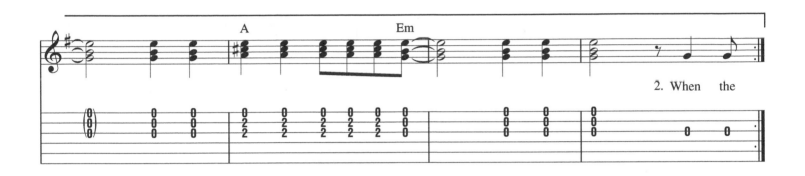

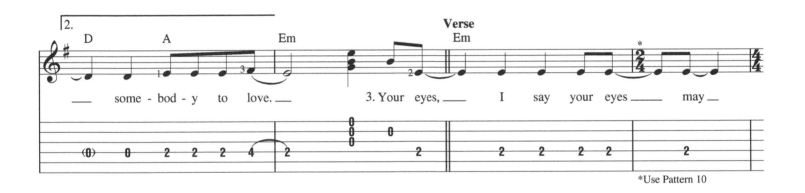

*Use Pattern 10

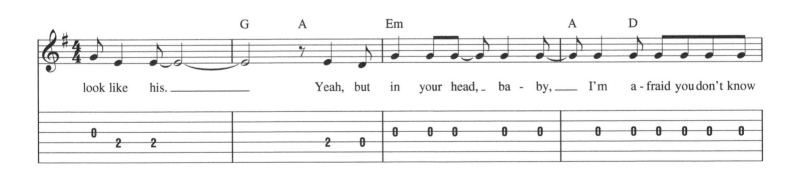

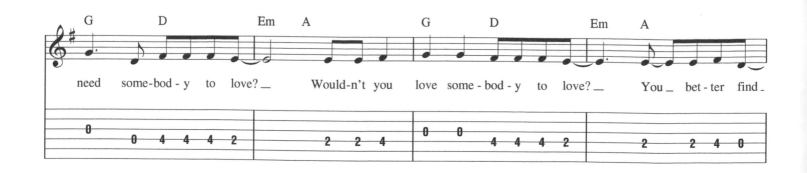

need some-bod-y to love?__ Would-n't you love some-bod-y to love?__ You__ bet-ter find__

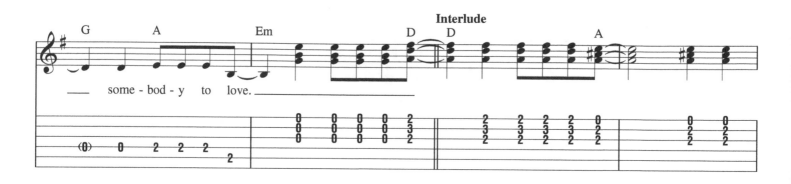

__ some-bod-y to love. _____ **Interlude**

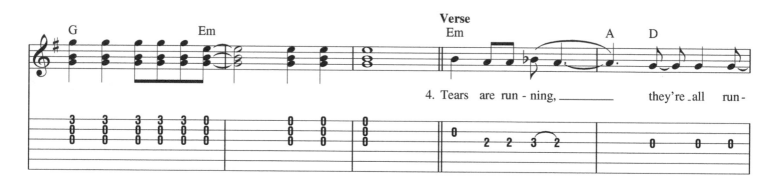

Verse

4. Tears are run-ning, _____ they're _all run-

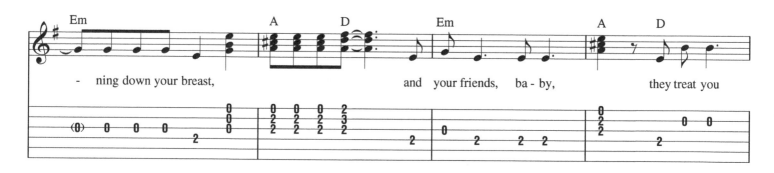

- ning down your breast, and your friends, ba-by, they treat you

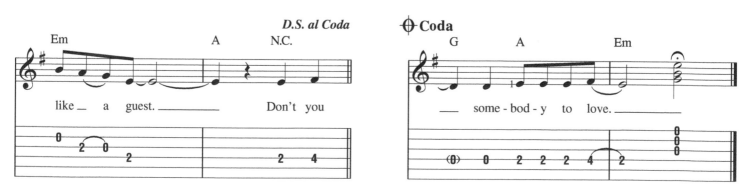

D.S. al Coda **Coda**

like __ a guest. _____ Don't you __ some-bod-y to love. _____

Additional Lyrics

2. When the garden flowers,
   Baby, are dead.
   Yes, and your mind, your mind
   Is so full of red.

Wonderwall

Words and Music by Noel Gallagher

Copyright © 1995 Sony Music Publishing United Kingdom and Creation Songs Ltd.
All Rights Administered by Sony/ATV Music Publishing LLC, 8 Music Square West, Nashville, TN 37203
International Copyright Secured   All Rights Reserved

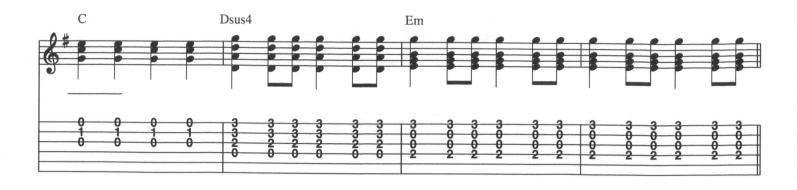

Verse

2. Back - beat the word was on the street that the fire ___ in your heart is out. ___
3. *See additional lyrics*

I'm sure you've heard it all be - fore but you

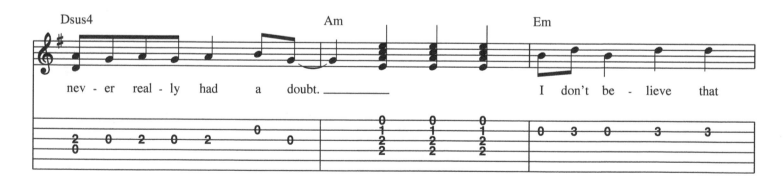

nev - er real - ly had a doubt. ___ I don't be - lieve that

an - y - bod - y ___ feels the way I do ___ a - bout you now. ___

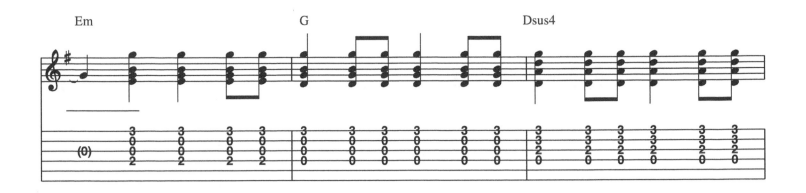

Pre-Chorus

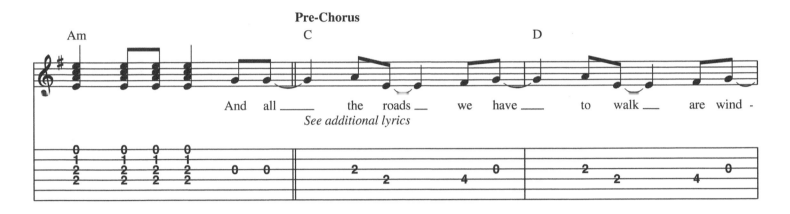

And all _____ the roads _____ we have _____ to walk _____ are wind -
See additional lyrics

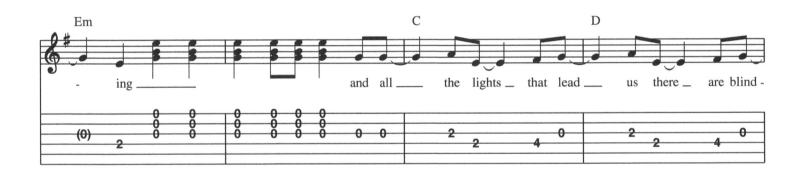

- ing _____ and all _____ the lights _ that lead _____ us there _ are blind -

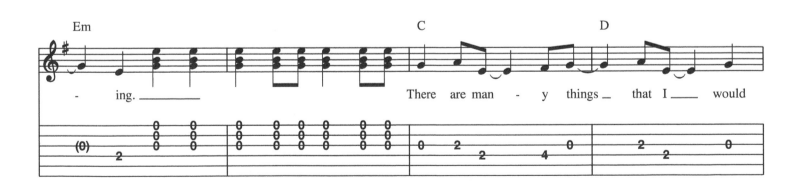

- ing. _____ There are man - y things _ that I _____ would

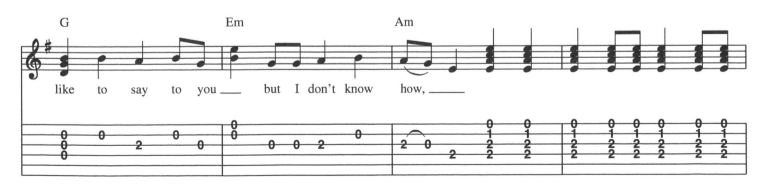

like to say to you _____ but I don't know how, _____

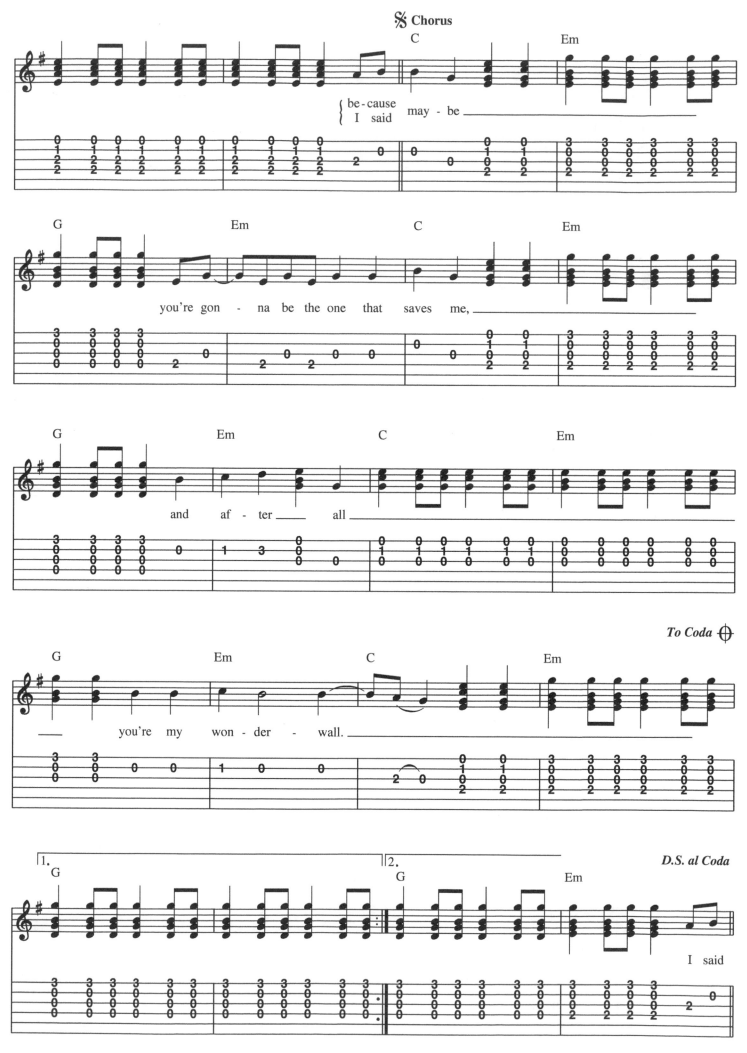

Additional Lyrics

3. Today was gonna be the day
   But they'll never throw it back to you.
   By now you should've somehow
   Realised what you're not to do.
   I don't believe that anybody
   Feels the way I do
   About you now.

Pre-Chorus And all the roads that lead you there were winding
   And all the lights that light the way are blinding.
   There are many things that I would like to say to you
   But I don't know how.

Suite: Judy Blue Eyes

Words and Music by Stephen Stills

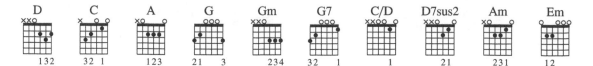

Strum Pattern: 2
Pick Pattern: 4

get-ting   to   the   point   where   I'm   no ____   fun   an - y - more.
2., 4. See additional lyrics

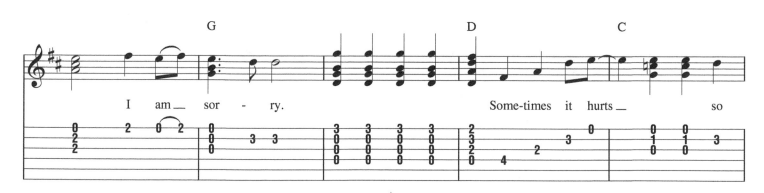

I   am __   sor - ry.   Some-times   it   hurts __   so

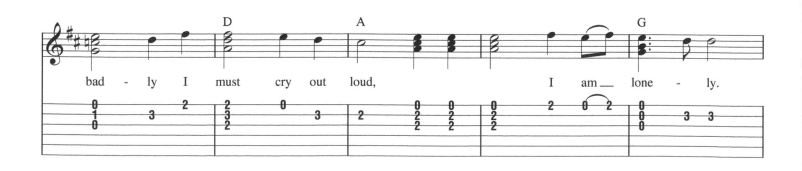

bad - ly   I   must   cry   out   loud,   I   am __   lone - ly.

Copyright © 1970 Gold Hill Music
Copyright Renewed
International Copyright Secured   All Rights Reserved

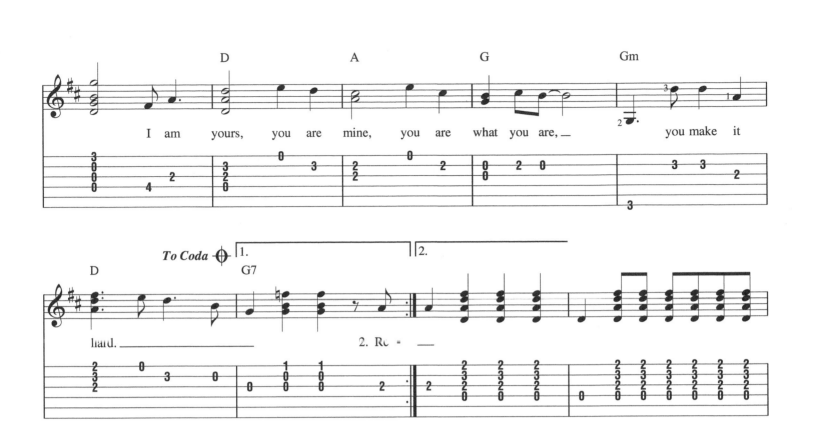

I am yours, you are mine, you are what you are, ___ you make it

To Coda ⊕ |1.
|2.

hard. _____ 2. Ru ___

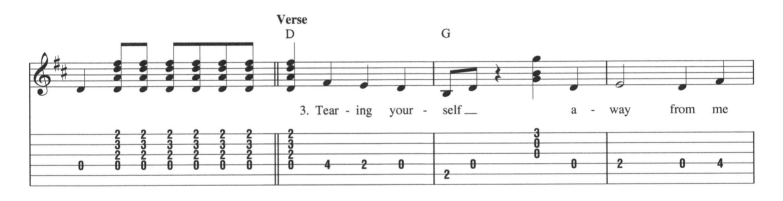

Verse

3. Tear - ing your - self ___ a - way from me

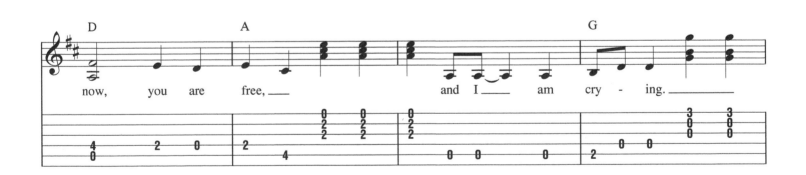

now, you are free, ___ and I ___ am cry - ing. _____

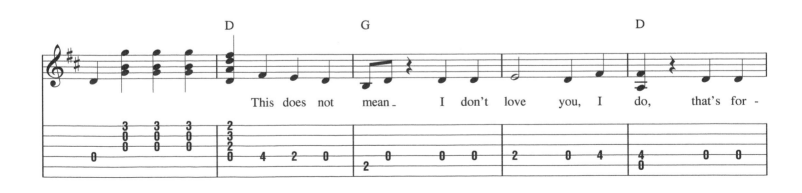

This does not mean ___ I don't love you, I do, that's for -

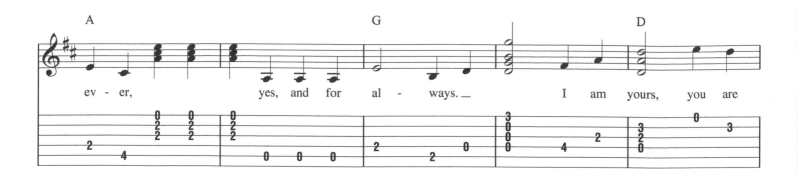

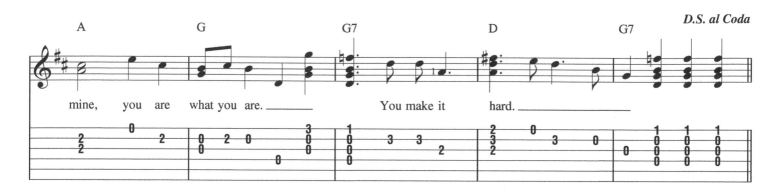

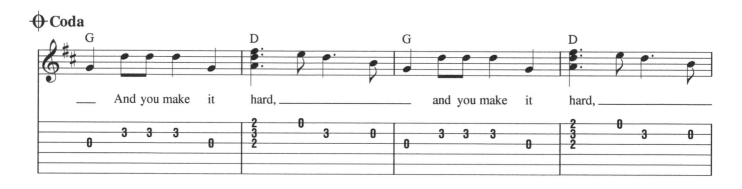

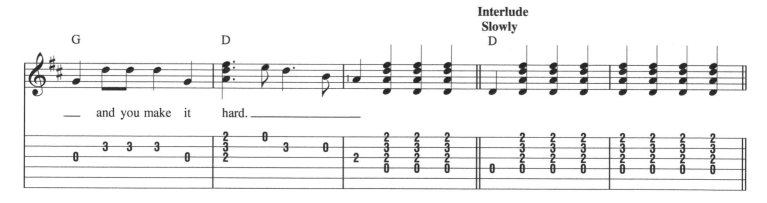

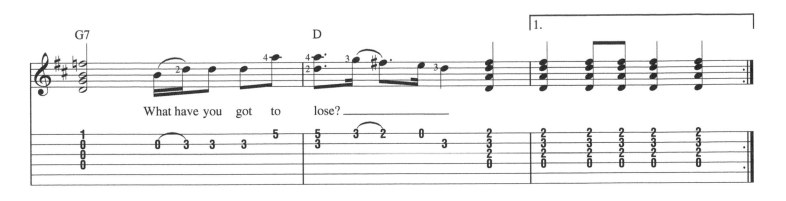

What have you got to lose? _____

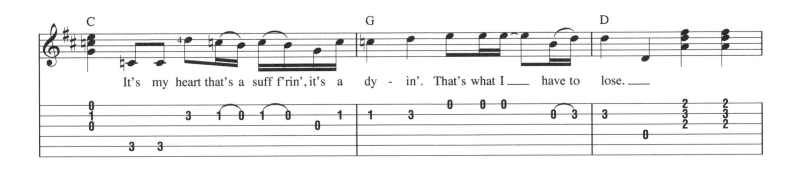

Can I tell it like it is? _____ Lis-ten to me ba - by.

It's my heart that's a suff'rin', it's a dy - in'. That's what I ____ have to lose. ____

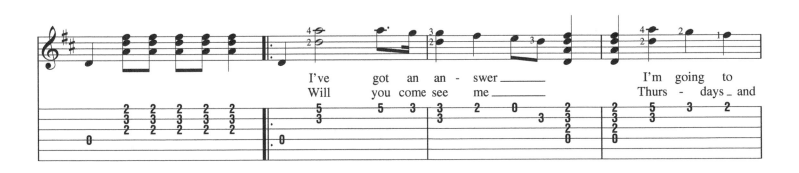

I've got an an - swer _____ I'm going to
Will you come see me _____ Thurs - days _ and

fly a - way. _
Sat - ur - days? _

What have I got to lose? _____
What have you got to lose? _____

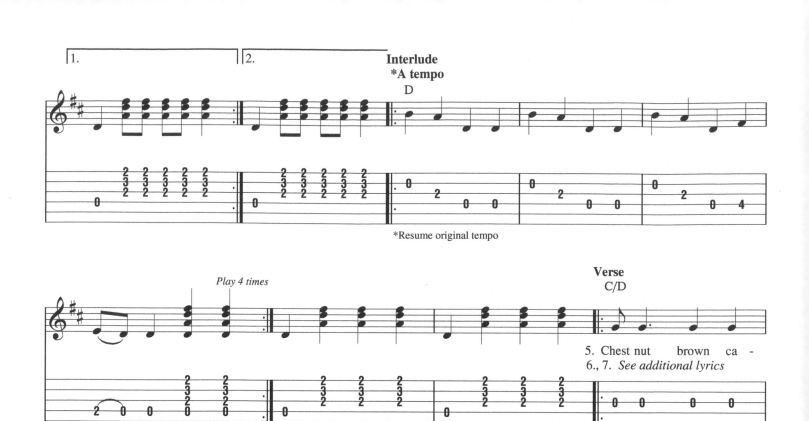

*Resume original tempo

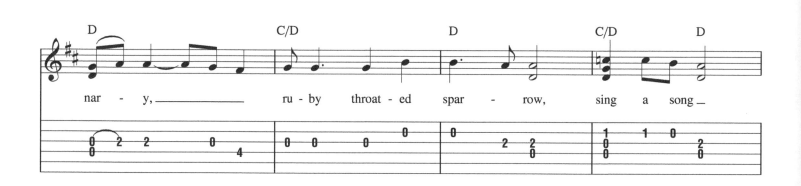

Play 4 times

Verse
C/D

5. Chest nut   brown ca -
6., 7. *See additional lyrics*

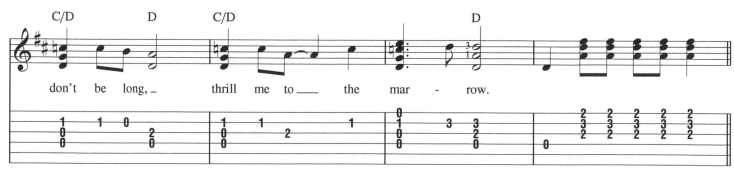

nar - y, _____ ru - by throat - ed spar - row, sing a song __

don't be long, __ thrill me to __ the mar - row.

1., 2.
Interlude

Additional Lyrics

2. Remember what we've said and done and felt about each other.
   Oh babe, have mercy.
   Don't let the past remind us of what we are not now.
   I am not dreaming.
   I am yours, you are mine, you are what you are.
   You make it hard.

4. Something inside is telling me that I've got your secret.
   Are you still list'ning?
   Fear is the lock and laughter the key to your heart.
   And I love you.
   I am yours, you are mine, you are what you are.
   You make it hard.
   And you make it hard.

6. Voices of the angels,
   Ring around the moonlight,
   Asking me, said she's so free,
   "How can you catch the sparrow?"

7. Lacy, lilting lyric,
   Losing love, lamenting,
   Change my life, make it right,
   Be my lady.

Time in a Bottle

Words and Music by Jim Croce

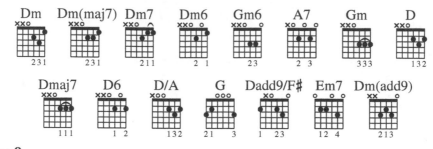

Strum Pattern: 9
Pick Pattern: 9

Intro
Moderately

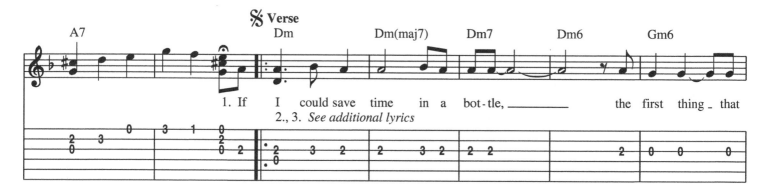

1. If I could save time in a bot-tle, _____ the first thing _ that
2., 3. *See additional lyrics*

I'd like to do. _____ is to save ev-'ry day till e-ter-ni-ty pass-es a-way just to

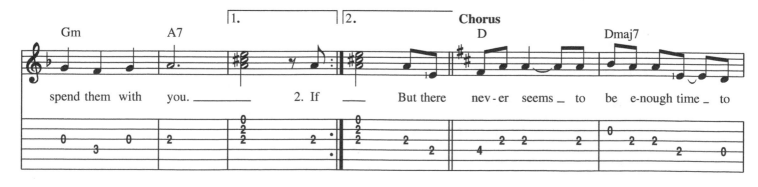

spend them with you. _____ 2. If _____ But there nev-er seems _ to be e-nough time _ to

© 1971 (Renewed 1999) TIME IN A BOTTLE PUBLISHING and CROCE PUBLISHING
All Rights Controlled and Administered by EMI APRIL MUSIC INC.
All Rights Reserved International Copyright Secured Used by Permission

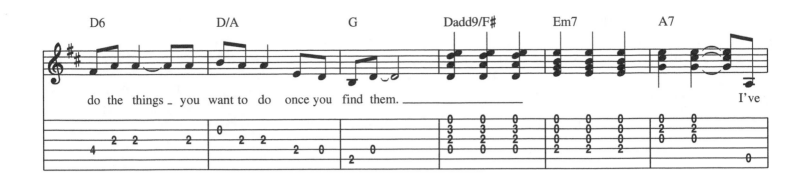

do the things _ you want to do once you find them. _____ I've

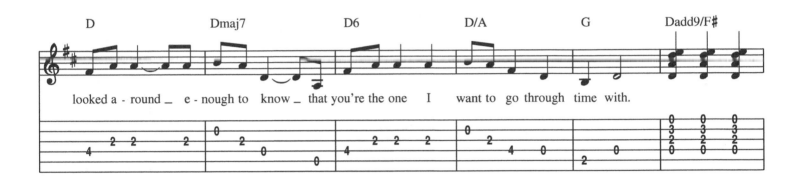

looked a - round _ e - nough to know _ that you're the one   I   want to go through time with.

Interlude

To Coda ⊕

D.S. al Coda
(take 2nd ending)

⊕ **Coda**
Outro

Play 3 times

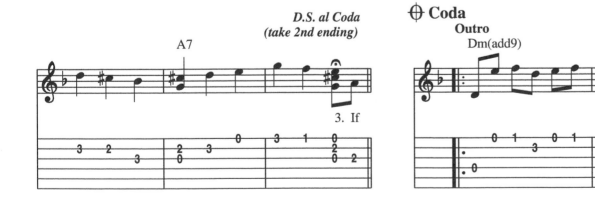

3. If

Additional Lyrics

2. If I could make days last forever,
   If words could make wishes come true,
   I'd save ev'ry day like a treasure, and then
   Again I would spend them with you.

3. If I had a box just for wishes,
   And dreams that had never come true,
   The box would be empty except for the mem'ry
   Of how they were answered by you.

HAL•LEONARD
GUITAR
PLAY-ALONG

INCLUDES TAB AUDIO ACCESS INCLUDED

This series will help you play your favorite songs quickly and easily. Just follow the tab and listen to the audio to hear how the guitar should sound, and then play along using the separate backing tracks.

Playback tools are provided for slowing down the tempo without changing pitch and looping challenging parts. The melody and lyrics are included in the book so that you can sing or simply follow along.

1. ROCK
00699570.................$16.99

2. ACOUSTIC
00699569.................$16.99

3. HARD ROCK
00699573.................$17.99

4. POP/ROCK
00699571.................$16.99

5. THREE CHORD SONGS
00300985.................$16.99

6. '90S ROCK
00298615.................$16.99

7. BLUES
00699575.................$17.99

8. ROCK
00699585.................$16.99

9. EASY ACOUSTIC SONGS
00151708.................$16.99

10. ACOUSTIC
00699586.................$16.95

11. EARLY ROCK
0699579.................$15.99

12. ROCK POP
00291724.................$16.99

14. BLUES ROCK
00699582.................$16.99

15. R&B
00699583.................$17.99

16. JAZZ
00699584.................$16.99

17. COUNTRY
00699588.................$16.99

18. ACOUSTIC ROCK
00699577.................$15.95

20. ROCKABILLY
00699580.................$16.99

21. SANTANA
00174525.................$17.99

22. CHRISTMAS
00699600.................$15.99

23. SURF
00699635.................$16.99

24. ERIC CLAPTON
00699649.................$17.99

25. THE BEATLES
00198265.................$17.99

26. ELVIS PRESLEY
00699643.................$16.99

27. DAVID LEE ROTH
00699645.................$16.95

28. GREG KOCH
00699646.................$17.99

29. BOB SEGER
00699647.................$16.99

30. KISS
00699644.................$16.99

32. THE OFFSPRING
00699653.................$14.95

33. ACOUSTIC CLASSICS
00699656.................$17.99

34. CLASSIC ROCK
00699658.................$17.99

35. HAIR METAL
00699660.................$17.99

36. SOUTHERN ROCK
00699661.................$19.99

37. ACOUSTIC UNPLUGGED
00699662.................$22.99

38. BLUES
00699663.................$17.99

39. '80S METAL
00699664.................$17.99

40. INCUBUS
00699668.................$17.95

41. ERIC CLAPTON
00699669.................$17.99

42. COVER BAND HITS
00211597.................$16.99

43. LYNYRD SKYNYRD
00699681.................$19.99

44. JAZZ GREATS
00699689.................$16.99

45. TV THEMES
00699718.................$14.95

46. MAINSTREAM ROCK
00699722.................$16.95

47. HENDRIX SMASH HITS
00699723.................$19.99

48. AEROSMITH CLASSICS
00699724.................$17.99

49. STEVIE RAY VAUGHAN
00699725.................$17.99

50. VAN HALEN 1978-1984
00110269.................$19.99

51. ALTERNATIVE '90S
00699727.................$14.99

52. FUNK
00699728.................$15.99

53. DISCO
00699729.................$14.99

54. HEAVY METAL
00699730.................$17.99

55. POP METAL
00699731.................$14.95

57. GUNS N' ROSES
00159922.................$17.99

58. BLINK-182
00699772.................$14.95

59. CHET ATKINS
00702347.................$16.99

60. 3 DOORS DOWN
00699774.................$14.95

62. CHRISTMAS CAROLS
00699798.................$12.95

63. CREEDENCE CLEARWATER REVIVAL
00699802.................$16.99

64. OZZY OSBOURNE
00699803.................$17.99

66. THE ROLLING STONES
00699807.................$17.99

67. BLACK SABBATH
00699808.................$16.99

68. PINK FLOYD – DARK SIDE OF THE MOON
00699809.................$17.99

71. CHRISTIAN ROCK
00699824.................$14.95

72. ACOUSTIC '90S
00699827.................$14.95

73. BLUESY ROCK
00699829.................$16.99

74. SIMPLE STRUMMING SONGS
00151706.................$19.99

75. TOM PETTY
00699882.................$19.99

76. COUNTRY HITS
00699884.................$16.99

77. BLUEGRASS
00699910.................$17.99

78. NIRVANA
00700132.................$16.99

79. NEIL YOUNG
00700133.................$24.99

80. ACOUSTIC ANTHOLOGY
00700175.................$19.95

81. ROCK ANTHOLOGY
00700176.................$22.99

82. EASY ROCK SONGS
00700177.................$17.99

84. STEELY DAN
00700200.................$19.99

85. THE POLICE
00700269.................$16.99

86. BOSTON
00700465.................$16.99

87. ACOUSTIC WOMEN
00700763.................$14.99

88. GRUNGE
00700467.................$16.99

89. REGGAE
00700468.................$15.99

90. CLASSICAL POP
00700469.................$14.99

91. BLUES INSTRUMENTALS
00700505.................$17.99

92. EARLY ROCK INSTRUMENTALS
00700506.................$15.99

93. ROCK INSTRUMENTALS
00700507.................$16.99

94. SLOW BLUES
00700508.................$16.99

95. BLUES CLASSICS
00700509.................$15.99

96. BEST COUNTRY HITS
00211615.................$16.99

97. CHRISTMAS CLASSICS
00236542.................$14.99

98. ROCK BAND
00700704.................$14.95

99. ZZ TOP
00700762.................$16.99

100. B.B. KING
00700466.................$16.99

101. SONGS FOR BEGINNERS
00701917.................$14.99

102. CLASSIC PUNK
00700769.................$14.99

103. SWITCHFOOT
00700773.................$16.99

104. DUANE ALLMAN
00700846.................$17.99

105. LATIN
00700939.........................$16.99

106. WEEZER
00700958.........................$14.99

107. CREAM
00701069.........................$16.99

108. THE WHO
00701053.........................$16.99

109. STEVE MILLER
00701054.........................$19.99

110. SLIDE GUITAR HITS
00701055.........................$16.99

111. JOHN MELLENCAMP
00701056.........................$14.99

112. QUEEN
00701052.........................$16.99

113. JIM CROCE
00701058.........................$17.99

114. BON JOVI
00701060.........................$16.99

115. JOHNNY CASH
00701070.........................$16.99

116. THE VENTURES
00701124.........................$17.99

117. BRAD PAISLEY
00701224.........................$16.99

118. ERIC JOHNSON
00701353.........................$16.99

119. AC/DC CLASSICS
00701356.........................$17.99

120. PROGRESSIVE ROCK
00701457.........................$14.99

121. U2
00701508.........................$16.99

122. CROSBY, STILLS & NASH
00701610.........................$16.99

123. LENNON & McCARTNEY ACOUSTIC
00701614.........................$16.99

124. SMOOTH JAZZ
00200664.........................$16.99

125. JEFF BECK
00701687.........................$17.99

126. BOB MARLEY
00701701.........................$17.99

127. 1970S ROCK
00701739.........................$16.99

128. 1960S ROCK
00701740.........................$14.99

129. MEGADETH
00701741.........................$17.99

130. IRON MAIDEN
00701742.........................$17.99

131. 1990S ROCK
00701743.........................$14.99

132. COUNTRY ROCK
00701757.........................$15.99

133. TAYLOR SWIFT
00701894.........................$16.99

134. AVENGED SEVENFOLD
00701906.........................$16.99

135. MINOR BLUES
00151350.........................$17.99

136. GUITAR THEMES
00701922.........................$14.99

137. IRISH TUNES
00701966.........................$15.99

138. BLUEGRASS CLASSICS
00701967.........................$17.99

139. GARY MOORE
00702370.........................$16.99

140. MORE STEVIE RAY VAUGHAN
00702396.........................$17.99

141. ACOUSTIC HITS
00702401.........................$16.99

142. GEORGE HARRISON
00237697.........................$17.99

143. SLASH
00702425.........................$19.99

144. DJANGO REINHARDT
00702531.........................$16.99

145. DEF LEPPARD
00702532.........................$19.99

146. ROBERT JOHNSON
00702533.........................$16.99

147. SIMON & GARFUNKEL
14041591.........................$16.99

148. BOB DYLAN
14041592.........................$16.99

149. AC/DC HITS
14041593.........................$17.99

150. ZAKK WYLDE
02501717.........................$19.99

151. J.S. BACH
02501730.........................$16.99

152. JOE BONAMASSA
02501751.........................$19.99

153. RED HOT CHILI PEPPERS
00702990.........................$19.99

155. ERIC CLAPTON – FROM THE ALBUM UNPLUGGED
00703085.........................$16.99

156. SLAYER
00703770.........................$19.99

157. FLEETWOOD MAC
00101382.........................$17.99

159. WES MONTGOMERY
00102593.........................$19.99

160. T-BONE WALKER
00102641.........................$17.99

161. THE EAGLES – ACOUSTIC
00102659.........................$17.99

162. THE EAGLES HITS
00102667.........................$17.99

163. PANTERA
00103036.........................$17.99

164. VAN HALEN 1986-1995
00110270.........................$17.99

165. GREEN DAY
00210343.........................$17.99

166. MODERN BLUES
00700764.........................$16.99

167. DREAM THEATER
00111938.........................$24.99

168. KISS
00113421.........................$17.99

169. TAYLOR SWIFT
00115982.........................$16.99

170. THREE DAYS GRACE
00117337.........................$16.99

171. JAMES BROWN
00117420.........................$16.99

172. THE DOOBIE BROTHERS
00116970.........................$16.99

173. TRANS-SIBERIAN ORCHESTRA
00119907.........................$19.99

174. SCORPIONS
00122119.........................$16.99

175. MICHAEL SCHENKER
00122127.........................$17.99

176. BLUES BREAKERS WITH JOHN MAYALL & ERIC CLAPTON
00122132.........................$19.99

177. ALBERT KING
00123271.........................$16.99

178. JASON MRAZ
00124165.........................$17.99

179. RAMONES
00127073.........................$16.99

180. BRUNO MARS
00129706.........................$16.99

181. JACK JOHNSON
00129854.........................$16.99

182. SOUNDGARDEN
00138161.........................$17.99

183. BUDDY GUY
00138240.........................$17.99

184. KENNY WAYNE SHEPHERD
00138258.........................$17.99

185. JOE SATRIANI
00139457.........................$17.99

186. GRATEFUL DEAD
00139459.........................$17.99

187. JOHN DENVER
00140839.........................$17.99

188. MÖTLEY CRUE
00141145.........................$17.99

189. JOHN MAYER
00144350.........................$17.99

190. DEEP PURPLE
00146152.........................$17.99

191. PINK FLOYD CLASSICS
00146164.........................$17.99

192. JUDAS PRIEST
00151352.........................$17.99

193. STEVE VAI
00156028.........................$19.99

194. PEARL JAM
00157925.........................$17.99

195. METALLICA: 1983-1988
00234291.........................$19.99

196. METALLICA: 1991-2016
00234292.........................$19.99

HAL•LEONARD®

For complete songlists, visit
Hal Leonard online at
www.halleonard.com

Prices, contents, and availability subject to
change without notice.
1120
9/12; 397

EASY GUITAR
WITH NOTES & TAB

This series features simplified arrangements with notes, tab, chord charts, and strum and pick patterns.

MIXED FOLIOS

00702287	Acoustic	$19.99
00702002	Acoustic Rock Hits for Easy Guitar	$15.99
00702166	All-Time Best Guitar Collection	$19.99
00702232	Best Acoustic Songs for Easy Guitar	$16.99
00119835	Best Children's Songs	$16.99
00703055	The Big Book of Nursery Rhymes & Children's Songs	$16.99
00698978	Big Christmas Collection	$19.99
00702394	Bluegrass Songs for Easy Guitar	$15.99
00289632	Bohemian Rhapsody	$19.99
00703387	Celtic Classics	$14.99
00224808	Chart Hits of 2016-2017	$14.99
00267383	Chart Hits of 2017-2018	$14.99
00334293	Chart Hits of 2019-2020	$16.99
00702149	Children's Christian Songbook	$9.99
00702028	Christmas Classics	$8.99
00101779	Christmas Guitar	$14.99
00702141	Classic Rock	$8.95
00159642	Classical Melodies	$12.99
00253933	Disney/Pixar's Coco	$16.99
00702203	CMT's 100 Greatest Country Songs	$34.99
00702283	The Contemporary Christian Collection	$16.99
00196954	Contemporary Disney	$19.99
00702239	Country Classics for Easy Guitar	$24.99

00702257	Easy Acoustic Guitar Songs	$16.99
00702041	Favorite Hymns for Easy Guitar	$12.99
00222701	Folk Pop Songs	$17.99
00126894	Frozen	$14.99
00333922	Frozen 2	$14.99
00702286	Glee	$16.99
00702160	The Great American Country Songbook	$19.99
00702148	Great American Gospel for Guitar	$14.99
00702050	Great Classical Themes for Easy Guitar	$9.99
00275088	The Greatest Showman	$17.99
00148030	Halloween Guitar Songs	$14.99
00702273	Irish Songs	$12.99
00192503	Jazz Classics for Easy Guitar	$16.99
00702275	Jazz Favorites for Easy Guitar	$17.99
00702274	Jazz Standards for Easy Guitar	$19.99
00702162	Jumbo Easy Guitar Songbook	$24.99
00232285	La La Land	$16.99
00702258	Legends of Rock	$14.99
00702189	MTV's 100 Greatest Pop Songs	$34.99
00702272	1950s Rock	$16.99
00702271	1960s Rock	$16.99
00702270	1970s Rock	$19.99
00702269	1980s Rock	$15.99
00702268	1990s Rock	$19.99
00369043	Rock Songs for Kids	$14.99

00109725	Once	$14.99
00702187	Selections from O Brother Where Art Thou?	$19.99
00702178	100 Songs for Kids	$14.99
00702515	Pirates of the Caribbean	$17.99
00702125	Praise and Worship for Guitar	$14.99
00287930	Songs from *A Star Is Born, The Greatest Showman, La La Land,* and More Movie Musicals	$16.99
00702285	Southern Rock Hits	$12.99
00156420	Star Wars Music	$16.99
00121535	30 Easy Celtic Guitar Solos	$16.99
00702156	3-Chord Rock	$12.99
00244654	Top Hits of 2017	$14.99
00283786	Top Hits of 2018	$14.99
00702294	Top Worship Hits	$17.99
00702255	VH1's 100 Greatest Hard Rock Songs	$34.99
00702175	VH1's 100 Greatest Songs of Rock and Roll	$29.99
00702253	Wicked	$12.99

ARTIST COLLECTIONS

00702267	AC/DC for Easy Guitar	$16.99
00702598	Adele for Easy Guitar	$15.99
00156221	Adele – 25	$16.99
00702040	Best of the Allman Brothers	$16.99
00702865	J.S. Bach for Easy Guitar	$15.99
00702169	Best of The Beach Boys	$15.99
00702292	The Beatles — 1	$22.99
00125796	Best of Chuck Berry	$15.99
00702201	The Essential Black Sabbath	$15.99
00702250	blink-182 — Greatest Hits	$17.99
02501615	Zac Brown Band — The Foundation	$17.99
02501621	Zac Brown Band — You Get What You Give	$16.99
00702043	Best of Johnny Cash	$17.99
00702090	Eric Clapton's Best	$16.99
00702086	Eric Clapton — from the Album Unplugged	$17.99
00702202	The Essential Eric Clapton	$17.99
00702053	Best of Patsy Cline	$15.99
00222697	Very Best of Coldplay – 2nd Edition	$16.99
00702229	The Very Best of Creedence Clearwater Revival	$16.99
00702145	Best of Jim Croce	$16.99
00702278	Crosby, Stills & Nash	$12.99
14042809	Bob Dylan	$15.99
00702276	Fleetwood Mac — Easy Guitar Collection	$17.99
00139462	The Very Best of Grateful Dead	$16.99
00702136	Best of Merle Haggard	$16.99
00702227	Jimi Hendrix — Smash Hits	$19.99
00702288	Best of Hillsong United	$12.99
00702236	Best of Antonio Carlos Jobim	$15.99
00702245	Elton John — Greatest Hits 1970–2002	$19.99

00129855	Jack Johnson	$16.99
00702204	Robert Johnson	$14.99
00702234	Selections from Toby Keith — 35 Biggest Hits	$12.95
00702003	Kiss	$16.99
00702216	Lynyrd Skynyrd	$16.99
00702182	The Essential Bob Marley	$16.99
00146081	Maroon 5	$14.99
00121925	Bruno Mars – Unorthodox Jukebox	$12.99
00702248	Paul McCartney — All the Best	$14.99
00125484	The Best of MercyMe	$12.99
00702209	Steve Miller Band — Young Hearts (Greatest Hits)	$12.95
00124167	Jason Mraz	$15.99
00702096	Best of Nirvana	$16.99
00702211	The Offspring — Greatest Hits	$17.99
00138026	One Direction	$17.99
00702030	Best of Roy Orbison	$17.99
00702144	Best of Ozzy Osbourne	$14.99
00702279	Tom Petty	$17.99
00102911	Pink Floyd	$17.99
00702139	Elvis Country Favorites	$19.99
00702293	The Very Best of Prince	$19.99
00699415	Best of Queen for Guitar	$16.99
00109279	Best of R.E.M.	$14.99
00702208	Red Hot Chili Peppers — Greatest Hits	$16.99
00198960	The Rolling Stones	$17.99
00174793	The Very Best of Santana	$16.99
00702196	Best of Bob Seger	$16.99
00146046	Ed Sheeran	$15.99
00702252	Frank Sinatra — Nothing But the Best	$12.99
00702010	Best of Rod Stewart	$17.99
00702049	Best of George Strait	$17.99

00702259	Taylor Swift for Easy Guitar	$15.99
00359800	Taylor Swift – Easy Guitar Anthology	$24.99
00702260	Taylor Swift — Fearless	$14.99
00139727	Taylor Swift — 1989	$17.99
00115960	Taylor Swift — Red	$16.99
00253667	Taylor Swift — Reputation	$17.99
00702290	Taylor Swift — Speak Now	$16.99
00232849	Chris Tomlin Collection – 2nd Edition	$14.99
00702226	Chris Tomlin — See the Morning	$12.95
00148643	Train	$14.99
00702427	U2 — 18 Singles	$19.99
00702108	Best of Stevie Ray Vaughan	$17.99
00279005	The Who	$14.99
00702123	Best of Hank Williams	$15.99
00194548	Best of John Williams	$14.99
00702228	Neil Young — Greatest Hits	$17.99
00119133	Neil Young — Harvest	$14.99

Prices, contents and availability subject to change without notice.

Visit Hal Leonard online at **halleonard.com**